BOOTS and BURGERS

AN ARIZONA Handbook FOR HUNGRY HIKERS

BY Roger Naylor

RIO NUEVO PUBLISHERS

Page ii: Sunbursts of wildflowers surround
backpackers on North Kaibab Trail.

Rio Nuevo Publishers®
P. O. Box 5250
Tucson, AZ 85703-0250
(520) 623-9558, www.rionuevo.com

Text © 2014 by Roger Naylor

Design: David Jenney Design
Cover Photo: Kerrick James

Library of Congress Cataloging-in-Publication Data

Naylor, Roger (Roger James), 1957-
  Boots & burgers : an Arizona handbook for hungry hikers / by Roger Naylor.
    pages cm
  ISBN 978-1-940322-00-1 (paperback) — ISBN 1-940322-00-6 (paperback)
1. Hiking—Arizona—Guidebooks. 2. Restaurants—Arizona—Guidebooks.
3. Arizona—Guidebooks. 4. Hamburgers—Arizona. I. Title.
  GV199.42.A7N39 2014
  796.5109791—dc23   2014016612

Printed in Korea

10   9   8   7   6   5   4   3   2   1

To

Eric Dickey,
Stuart Wright,

and especially

Martin Kuz.

Many favorite trails and tasty burgers

were shared with these hombres.

CONTENTS

page

1 **Introduction**
2 Hitting the Trail: Backcountry Safety and Etiquette
4 Weather
5 Getting Lost
5 Wildlife
6 Trail Etiquette

CHAPTER ONE *Flagstaff*

9 **1 Humphreys Peak Trail** } *Mama Burger, Flagstaff*
12 **2 Kachina Trail** } *Diablo Burger, Flagstaff*
14 **3 Red Mountain Trail** } *Miz Zip's, Flagstaff*
17 **4 Veit Springs Loop** } *Satchmo's, Flagstaff*

CHAPTER TWO *Sedona and the Verde Valley*

21 **5 Hangover Trail, Sedona** } *Cowboy Club, Sedona*
25 **6 Hiline Trail, Sedona** } *PJ's Village Pub & Sports Lounge, Sedona*
26 **7 Marg's Draw, Sedona** } *Simon's Hot Dogs, Sedona*
28 **8 West Fork Trail, Sedona** } *Garland's Indian Gardens Café & Market, Sedona*
32 **9 Parsons Trail, Clarkdale** } *Haunted Hamburger, Jerome*
35 **10 Thumper Loop, Cottonwood** } *Verde Lea Market Deli & Grill, Cottonwood*

CHAPTER THREE *Central Highlands*

39 **11 Salida Gulch Trail, Prescott** } *Bill's Grill, Prescott*
42 **12 Watson Lake Loop, Prescott** } *Brown Bag Burger, Prescott*
44 **13 Sycamore Rim, Williams** } *Twisters 50's Soda Fountain, Williams*

CHAPTER FOUR *Grand Canyon*

49 **14 Bright Angel – Tonto – South Kaibab Loop, South Rim**
     } *Bright Angel Soda Fountain, Grand Canyon Village*
53 **15 Grandview Trail, South Rim**
54 **16 North Kaibab Trail, North Rim** } *Grand Canyon Lodge*
59 **17 Widforss Trail, North Rim** } *Lees Ferry Lodge at Vermilion Cliffs, Marble Canyon*

CHAPTER FIVE *Utah Border*

63 **18 Hanging Garden Trail, Page** } *Ja'di''To'oh, Antelope Point Marina*
66 **19 Wildcat Trail, Monument Valley** } *The View Hotel, Monument Valley*

Continued ⟹

page   CHAPTER SIX *Phoenix and the Central Deserts*

69   **20   Cholla Trail, Camelback Mountain** } *Pizzeria Bianco, Phoenix*

71   **21   Freedom Trail, Piestewa Peak** } *Chicago Hamburger Company, Phoenix*

73   **22   North Trail, McDowell Mountains** } *Paradise Valley Burger Company, Phoenix*

75   **23   Siphon Draw, Superstition Mountains** } *The Chuckbox, Tempe*

77   **24   Vulture Peak, Wickenburg** } *Chaparral Homemade Ice Cream, Wickenburg*

80   **25   Wind Cave, Usery Mountains** } *Flancer's, Mesa*

CHAPTER SEVEN *Tucson and the Southern Deserts*

83   **26   Bear Canyon, Tucson** } *Pat's Drive-In, Tucson*

85   **27   Canyon Loop, Tucson** } *Sullivan's Eatery & Creamery, Tucson*

88   **28   Hugh Norris, Tucson** } *El Güero Canelo, Tucson*

89   **29   Cochise Trail, Sunsites** } *Horseshoe Café & Bakery, Benson*

91   **30   Heart of Rocks, Chiricahua National Monument** } *Jimmy's, Bisbee*

94   **31   Juan Bautista de Anza Trail, Tubac** } *Wisdom's Café, Tumacácori*

CHAPTER EIGHT *Arizona's West Coast*

97   **32   Crack-in-the-Mountain, Lake Havasu City** } *Sandbar & Grill, Lake Havasu City*
     Jersey's Grill, Lake Havasu City

99   **33   Monolith Garden Trail, Kingman** } *Redneck's Southern Pit Barbecue, Kingman*

102   **34   Telegraph Pass, Yuma** } *Lute's Casino*

CHAPTER NINE *Eastern High Country*

105   **35   Horton Creek, Payson** } *Buffalo Bar & Grill, Payson*

108   **36   Panorama Trail, Pinetop-Lakeside** } *The Lion's Den Bar & Grill, Pinetop*
     Moose Henri's, Lakeside

110   **37   West Baldy, Springerville-Eagar** } *TrailRiders Restaurant, Eagar*

115   **Acknowledgments**

116   **About the Author**

117   **Photo Credits**

Introduction

HERE'S THE SCENARIO: I roll out of bed and point my truck toward a trail. I hike into the Arizona outback under a high arched sky with a lingering hint of moonlight. Dawn wounds the eastern horizon as coyote yips recede in the distance.

I walk for miles. I wander lonesome lands—a maze of canyons, a canopied forest or a snarl of desert—it doesn't matter. I adore every square inch of this heart-wringing, soul-squeezing state. The silence soothes me. Wildlife swoops and scampers at the edge of my vision. The lustrous light of morning sharpens to a hard glare. The twisted trail pulls me deeper into wilderness as wildflowers perfume a subtle breeze. Past noon the sun turns squinty-eyed mean. The heat begins to stalk me with a knife in its teeth. I walk for miles.

On the drive home I stop at a diner or café, a casual joint where no one bats an eye at my dusty boots and sweat-streaked shirt. The waitress calls me "Hon" and hustles out my drinks. I don't need a menu because I know exactly what I want. I chug ice water and my stomach rumbles until my burger arrives. I bite into the grill-kissed slab of beef.

Right there, that's my favorite day of all. That's Halloween, Christmas, and the spring equinox

rolled into one. Walk off a few calories and then pack them on again. I admire the Zen-like simplicity of it. I'll take a boots and burgers day anytime I can get it.

Boots

Look in my closet and all you'll find are eight pairs of hiking boots, Merrell's Moab Ventilator, identical except for the varying stages of wear and tear. No sneakers, sandals, or flip-flops, just boots. I live in hiking boots.

Though I don't hike every day, I can. I'm always dressed for the trail. From my window I see mountains, mesas, and red rock cliffs. This is no place to hunker indoors. Easy access to trails and a user-friendly climate make Arizona a biped's paradise. If hiking isn't our official state pastime, it should be. A trail snatches you; steals you from the mundane. The common misnomer is that we take a trail. In reality, the trail takes us.

By putting boots to soil, pinning eyes on the horizon and plunging into wild country, we reap untold benefits, both healthy and spiritual. Walking has been described as controlled falling. Hiking, for me, is controlled falling in love.

Burgers

I turned outlaw during the third grade, a pint-sized desperado lured down a wicked path by a craving I couldn't control.

Twice a week I left elementary school to walk home for lunch, which was permitted as long as you went home. But I didn't. Instead I ducked into a dimly lit joint. I couldn't help myself; I was jonesing for the good stuff.

As soon as my tiny figure darkened the doorway, the man behind the counter knew what to do. He slapped a hamburger on the grill. Yes, I had a cow on my back. I was hooked on burgers. Let the other saps at school choke down a brick of institutional-grade meatloaf; I was feasting on a juicy joy bomb, the most exquisite of foods, the coup de grease . . . the burger.

A hamburger is the king of comfort food because it's a flashback on a bun. With the first bite you are transported to a more innocent time when your world revolved around simple pleasures like cartoons, running fast down a hill for no reason, and throwing rocks at someone you had a crush on, then refueling with a burger and a shake.

All these years later and burgers still hold me in their sway. They're the perfect post-hike meal, but to be clear, I do NOT eat a burger every time I go for a walk. I have reformed the bad habits of my youth. Moderation is the key. My vegetarian wife is a terrific cook and has broadened my culinary horizons considerably. I enjoy a wide range of foods. Yet I never lost my taste for the simple elegance of a hamburger. That familiar blast of charred but juicy meat, meshing with a chorus of complimentary flavors in an easy-to-chomp package still rocks my world. Now they are a treat, not a staple.

I'm an avid hiker, topping the 1,000-mile mark many years. Most days I eat pretty healthy, but once every week or two, I pounce on a burger. Or hot dog. Sometimes barbecue, or pizza, or burrito. Depends what trail I'm on. You'll find plenty of my favorite eateries here.

This book is a love letter to Arizona masquerading as a hiking and dining guide. Beyond trail descriptions and restaurant info, I provide suggestions for other local attractions and activities. I add historic tidbits, fast facts, rambling thoughts,

personal anecdotes, and big dollops of quirkiness. When you spend as much alone time on the trail as I do, all sorts of weird notions ricochet through the old noggin.

Most of all it's packed with great days, amazing days, my best days. Peel off a few for yourself. Lace up the boots and explore the scenic wonders of this epic landscape. Then unwind in a comfortable hideout, where burgers leap off the grill like trout from a stream. Let yourself be pampered by a spatula technician. Order a burger—cheese it if you want—and bite into your delicious past.

Want fries with that?

Hitting the Trail: Backcountry Safety and Etiquette

First things first, heed this word of warning. Hiking isn't typically dangerous. Yet any type of recreation carries certain risks. The very things that make it so enticing—you're outside, exposed to the elements, and far from civilization—also add aspects of danger. To ensure your safety, be prepared ahead of time and always stay alert while on the trail. Here are a few tips to keep you healthy, happy, and coming back for more.

Don't kid yourself. Be honest when assessing your physical capabilities. Don't hoist yourself off the couch and attempt to hike the Grand Canyon. Especially if "hoist" is an accurate assessment of what it takes to get you off the sofa. I've rated trails as easy, moderate, or strenuous. That's my subjective ranking factoring in distance, terrain, and elevation gain. If you can manage a few laps around the mall without wheezing, you should be able to handle easy ones. Moderate trails require a higher level of fitness because you'll be making some climbs or racking up the mileage. Strenuous trails are best suited for experienced hikers in good health.

Get the 411: Each trail in the book comes with the basics to get you started like directions to the trailhead, length of the trail, and difficulty rating. But it's important for you to acquire the latest information. That's why I include contact details for each hike. Check on current road and trail condi-

Bright Angel Trail zigzags past Three Mile Resthouse.

tions, which can change over time or be impacted by the seasons. And always get a weather forecast.

Join a gang. Hike with others. This rule I almost always break because I'm a crotchety old coot who prefers solitude. Wiser and more sociable folks can recruit friends or family, or join a hiking club.

Spill the beans. This is the big one, the cardinal rule. Always let someone know your hiking plans, where you're going, and when you'll return. Always.

Dress for success. Start with comfortable hiking boots. And when I say boots, don't picture stiff, boxy, all-leather models from the Frankenstein line of footwear. If a boot requires a lengthy "breaking in" period, keep shopping. You want lightweight but sturdy, a sneaker with attitude. Wear a wide-brimmed hat and slather on the sunscreen. Dress in layers. Temperatures can change dramatically through the day and at different elevations.

Drink up. By the time you feel thirsty you're already slightly dehydrated. Arizona's arid climate wrings you out much quicker than you realize. I always hydrate thoroughly before starting and drink steadily on the hike. For desert hiking, carry at least a gallon per day. And not just water. Longer hikes demand some electrolyte-replacement drinks. Even if you have a post-hike burger in your sights, munching a few salty snacks on the trail will keep your energy level up.

The right stuff. Carry a few essentials like a first aid kit, flashlight, compass, map, snacks, whistle, signal mirror, and knife. Plus, tweezers, comb, and duct tape, which are the primary tools of removing an array of cactus spines.

You talking to me? Carry a cell phone but don't rely on it. Getting a signal in the outback is never a sure thing. And don't be gabbing all loud and self-absorbed for no reason. Just because you're outside doesn't mean other trail users want to hear your outside voice.

Weather

You can hike year round in Arizona and, baby, that's just what I do. The best months for desert hiking are October through April. During the ferocious heat of summer, head for higher ground. Temperatures cool as elevation rises. While summer brutalizes the lower deserts, the forests of the high country stay ridiculously mild.

Arizona has two wet seasons. At least if our prayers are answered we do. Winter brings gentle widespread rains in the desert and snow in the high country. During the monsoon, or summer thunderstorm season, hard-pounding localized rains can erupt suddenly in afternoons. A shifting wind pattern draws warm, moist air from the Gulf of Mexico. Officially, monsoon season begins on June 15 and ends on September 30, with storms peaking between mid-July and mid-August, so always pack rain gear during this period. Keep yourself warm and dry to avoid hypothermia. And don't hesitate to turn back if weather turns menacing.

Thunderstorms are often accompanied by angry, boiling clouds and sky-scorching lightning. If you are caught in a lightning storm, don't seek shelter under large trees or rock outcroppings. Avoid ridgelines, peaks, and open spaces. Head for a low spot and crouch down, making yourself a small, uninteresting target.

Flash floods are another serious danger in Arizona. Water levels can rise suddenly even if it's not raining on your location. Storms upstream can send a wall of water through narrow canyons and normally dry washes can turn into raging rivers. Stay out of such places if rain is possible. The fury of flash floods happens quickly but doesn't last. Wait for waters to recede before crossing flooded arroyos. Likewise, don't attempt to drive across flooded roadways.

Getting Lost

This is an embarrassing admission for an experienced hiker but I have a terrible sense of direction. I can get lost on the way to my mailbox. Because I'm aware of this shortcoming, I study landmarks and terrain. All trails in this book are well-marked day hikes requiring no special route-finding skills. So going astray shouldn't be an issue. If you do wander off trail, stop immediately. Relax, look around, and assess your situation. In most cases you should be able to backtrack to the trail. Consult your map and compass if necessary. Blast away on your whistle to attract the attention of other hikers in the area. Phone for help if all else fails.

Wildlife

The backcountry of Arizona is home to a few venomous creatures such as scorpions, black widow spiders, Gila monsters, and rattlesnakes. To avoid any unpleasant encounters don't put hands or feet anywhere you can't see. When you find a log or boulder in the trail, don't step over in a single stride, just in case something is snoozing on the other side. Step up onto the log and then over, landing clear of the base.

Chances are you won't run into a rattlesnake on the trail and even if you do, they're not stalking you. Rattlers aren't aggressive and don't bite unless they feel threatened. If you are bitten, stay calm—which is easier said than done because you've just been bitten by a rattlesnake! Maybe this will help: rattlesnake bites are a serious medical emergency but generally not life threatening. Remove watches or rings, which may constrict swelling. Keep the wound below the heart and get to the hospital as quickly as possible.

The likelihood of meeting other potentially dangerous wildlife, such as black bears or mountain lions, is even more remote. If you do come face to face with one of the big animals, always keep a safe distance. Keep children close and dogs under control. Do not run. Make noise. In the extremely rare case that you are attacked, fight back.

TRAIL ETIQUETTE

☞ Pack out everything you pack in, no matter how small. If you happen to see trash left by some imbecile, don't just cluck your tongue in dismay. Haul it out with you.

☞ Stay on the trail. Short cuts and stray paths speed erosion and trample fragile plants.

☞ Don't disturb anything. Leave rocks, plants, and artifacts just as you find them.

☞ Hikers yield to equestrians. Bicyclists are supposed to yield to everyone, but, frankly, it's much easier for a hiker to step aside and let the biker breeze past. When approaching equestrians, speak up so the horse knows you're a person and not a well-disguised mountain lion. Then stand quietly to the side of the trail.

☞ Hikers traveling downhill should yield to uphill hikers. If the ascending hikers want to stop for a rest break, they can wave you through.

☞ Don't use a trail when it's wet. Trekking through the mud is not much fun anyway and can begin a process of erosion that's difficult to reverse. It's Arizona—the sun will pop out and dry the trail soon enough.

☞ Respect wildlife. Never feed or disturb critters you might encounter.

☞ To dispose of human waste, dig a hole four to six inches deep and at least a hundred yards from water sources and dry washes. Do not burn or bury toilet paper. Instead, pack it out in a plastic baggie.

☞ Before hiking with your dog, make sure pooches are allowed on that particular trail. Carry extra water and snacks. Always keep Marmaduke on a leash and pick up any trail deposits he might make.

"Between every two pine trees
there is a door leading to
a new way of life."

—JOHN MUIR

FLAGSTAFF

THE SAN FRANCISCO PEAKS, which form a scenic backdrop for the town of Flagstaff, are the hulking remains of an eroded stratovolcano. They're part of a volcanic belt stretching for fifty miles. In the 17th century, Spanish friars bestowed the name San Francisco to the mountains in honor of St. Francis of Assisi. It had nothing to do with the yet-to-exist burg by the bay where Tony Bennett so casually misplaced his ticker. As a freshman at Northern Arizona University, I was told the mountains acquired their name because you could see the lights of San Francisco from the summit. I was also warned that on cold nights, packs of wolves loped from the heights and prowled the streets in search of meat. Also not true. But to a gullible Ohio boy who had seen little beyond flat fields and farmlands, anything seemed possible in this dramatic landscape.

№ 1 Humphreys Peak Trail

The San Francisco Peaks are the sexiest mountains in the state. They're an intimate range with curving, seductive lines and a hint of the forbidden. A décolletage of tundra is visible above the tree line. How can you resist?

Flagstaff aspens get rowdy.

Humphreys Peak tops out at 12,633 feet, the highest point in the state. Other hiking guidebooks tout the spectacular views from the summit—and they are pretty eye-poppingly yowza. But I'll level with you; the vistas are hard to fully appreciate because the wind has a personal vendetta against hikers. It blows frequently, raking exposed ridges, rattling the stones, and doing everything possible to sweep you over the edge. This is not a hike you take for pure pleasure. You do it because you have a screw loose—because some crazy notion compels you to climb to the roof of Arizona.

From the trailhead, the route cuts across a meadow and enters a dense forest of spruce, fir, and aspen. The tangled canopy creates a tunnel effect so don't expect big panoramas early. The ascent isn't steep at first, just relentless. At the 11,400 feet mark there's a sign warning that camping is not permitted beyond this point. And who, besides Yeti, would even consider it? Things start getting serious from

Hot Tip The Flagstaff Ale Trail is a self-guided craft beer walking tour of downtown with multiple stops. It was created to promote local businesses and showcase the burgeoning craft beer scene in Flagstaff, which is—pardon the pun—hopping. www.flagstaffaletrail.com.

Crossing the stark tundra atop Humphreys Peak.

here. Switchbacks tighten, the grade sharpens, and the forest begins to break apart. Soon nothing is left but gnarled, twisted bristlecone pines. They're the toughest tree in the world, surviving impossibly harsh conditions, but soon even they say, "Screw it. You go ahead, we'll wait here."

At 11,800 feet you reach the saddle connecting Humphreys and Agassiz, the second-highest peak in the range. From this high perch there's a spectacular view into a rough-hewn valley filled with crumbling cliffs and scraps of forest. With a little more climbing, I'm above the tree line completely.

All that remains is a lung-squeezing slog across a raggedy ridge of alpine tundra, the only region of tundra found in Arizona. Tundra ecosystems are treeless regions found in the Arctic and at high elevations on mountains, where the climate is cold and windy. It is moonscape-stark up here, a jumble of dark rocks with a few shriveled plants growing in sheltered crannies. As I cross this barren spine, the wind batters and claws me, and the air is as thin as Olive Oyl on a juice diet.

Expect a couple of false summits—oh, cruel ridges—before bagging Humphreys. A parapet of lava rocks is stacked on the summit, allowing me a chance to hunker out of the wind and revel in the fact that for a while, I am the tallest person in

Arizona. When I do take a gander over the stones, I spot Grand Canyon, the Hopi Mesas, and the pastel cliffs of the Painted Desert.

Where: From Flagstaff, drive north on U.S. 180 for 7 miles to Forest Road 516 (Snowbowl Road). Turn right and continue 6.4 miles to the lower parking lot on the left.

Cost: Free.   **Difficulty:** Strenuous.

Length: 9.6 miles round-trip.

Details: (928) 526-0866, www.fs.usda.gov/coconino.

Mama Burger   FLAGSTAFF

If you love burgers, it's probably because of Mama Burger or a place just like it. Before fast-food joints corrupted the process, this was how we got our burger fix: someone in an apron tossing a ball of fresh meat onto the flattop. There's still magic in the simplicity of it. Burgers are made with pure Angus chuck and pressed once with a steak weight as they sizzle on the griddle. The process creates a thin, rough-hewn patty boasting a delicate crispness around the edges but sacrificing nothing in the juicy department. Swabbed with a house-made Thousand Island and stacked with fresh produce, these slender beauties are the Flagstaff version of In-N-Out. Of course, I opt for mustard instead of the sauce. Salad dressing and burgers don't mix as far as I'm concerned.

The sinfully addictive fresh-cut fries are among the best in the state, radiant with zesty spud flavor. They start the morning as potatoes and are hand cut and cooked in zero-trans-fat oil, seasoned, and served piping hot. You can even have them served atop your burger. If all mamas tried that, nobody would ever leave home. 991 N. Fort Valley Road, (928) 226-0616, www.themamaburger.com.

The bulky San Francisco Peaks loom over Flagstaff.

№2 Kachina Trail

This high country ramble delivers a big mountain experience without any real climbing, bless its woodsy heart. Kachina follows a gently rolling course across the midsection of the San Francisco Peaks. It passes through conifer groves and huddled aspens framed by slanted meadows filled with waist-high bracken ferns.

The trail stretches five miles, descending 700 feet from the upper end at 9,500 feet to its terminus in the mouth of Weatherford Canyon. Limber pine and Douglas fir dominate old growth forests at the highest elevations. As the trail drops to the south facing slopes of Agassiz and Fremont peaks, our old friends the ponderosa pines rise up in welcome.

Fast Fact: The San Francisco Peaks ragwort resembles a very tiny sunflower blooming amid the volcanic talus of the tundra. It grows there and nowhere else in the world.

Occasional meadows brush aside the trees along Kachina Trail. **Right:** An inviting forest swaddles Kachina Trail.

Although popular, the trail seldom feels overrun. Everyone seems to find a comfortable pace and strings out among the trees. As a card-carrying curmudgeon, I tend to steer clear of crowds but have never gotten cranky on Kachina. Clusters of andesite boulders, remnants of an ancient lava flow, are scattered through the timber. Such a peaceful landscape, it's hard to believe it was born of fire. The river of lava that once scoured these slopes has been embraced by the forest, which seems to bear no grudge. Big boulders are sprinkled with soil, leaves, and debris, and trees grow from their very pores.

Dipping in and out of shallow drainages and skirting small cliffs, I wind around the rising bulk of the peaks. On the second half of the hike, the pastures widen exposing lovely views of mountaintops above and towns, buttes, and hills far below.

When the Kachina junctions with the Weatherford Trail, about-face it and return to your car. This is one of those ideal hikes where you'll enjoy the going as much as the coming.

Where: Drive 7 miles northwest of Flagstaff on U.S. 180 and turn right on Snowbowl Road. Follow the road about 6.4 miles to the ski area. Turn into the first parking area on the right.

Cost: Free.   **Difficulty:** Moderate.

Length: 10 miles round-trip.

Details: (928) 526-0866, www.fs.usda.gov/coconino.

PONDEROSA PINES Someone bakes cookies in the forests of Northern Arizona. At least that's what it smells like. Maybe it's Keebler elves, or possibly unaffiliated scab elves. But when you're hiking on a sunny day you often catch the scent of vanilla. Or is it butterscotch?

Lean in close to the tree and the aroma grabs you by your olfactory lapels and shakes you. But don't bother looking for a knothole where you can stuff dollar bills and order a sack of warm pecan sandies. It's the ponderosa pines themselves emitting the perfume of vanilla. Although some people claim it smells more like butterscotch.

The ponderosa pine is one of the Southwest's tallest trees, growing to heights of more than 200 feet, with trunks three-to-four feet across. They make a majestic forest, and when you stick your nose into a crevice of the bark, it is a little whiff of heaven, the rich fragrance of vanilla. Or is it butterscotch?

Diablo Burger FLAGSTAFF

Before you bite into one of the delectable slabs of beef at Diablo Burger, you're probably thinking, Why is it cradled on an English muffin? After much experimentation, DB decided the light, crisp muffin makes the perfect wrapping for the burger. With meat this fresh and tender, you want just the right framework. All burgers are made using open-range, antibiotic-free beef from Diablo Trust ranches, operating southeast of Flagstaff. This arrangement supports the stewardship of nearly a half million acres of a local ecosystem.

Since the beef is about 95 percent lean, try it medium-rare. This is an excellent burger, but as a traditionalist I do not graciously embrace change. On the standard burger, I'm slightly distracted by the muffin. But it probably works better with more complex creations. And here's a tip: Put the lettuce between the tomato and top of the English muffin. That keeps the moisture of the tomato from turning the muffin soggy. They serve frites, or Belgian-style fries, fresh cut, cooked twice in peanut oil and seasoned with a dash of rosemary. Delicious! 120 N. Leroux St., (928) 774-3274, www.diabloburger.com.

The gnawed hoodoos of Red Mountain.

№ 3 Red Mountain Trail

I love the fantasyland aspect of Red Mountain and the sudden jangly weirdness of it. The short, easy trail travels through scenic woodlands before plunging into the mystical gullet of a volcano.

Red Mountain is one of several hundred cinder cones that poke through every pore in the volcanic landscape surrounding Flagstaff. But unlike most symmetrical cones, Red Mountain is a haphazard U-shape, with an amphitheater carved from the northeast flank. "Carved" may mislead; it looks like some giant cosmic being took a chomp, leaving behind a raggedy assortment of hoodoos and a labyrinth of slender canyons.

The trail starts on a wide path rising gently through a forest of junipers and piñon pines. Dipping into a sandy wash it continues toward the base of Red Mountain, which towers 1,000 feet overhead. So far everything seems normal, but a mile from the trailhead, things take a turn for the freaky.

Walls of black cinder rise up, flanking the streambed with a few lonely ponderosa pines growing from the desolation. The trail squeezes between dark towers of volcanic tuff (ash that's

Entering the cinder-coated weirdness of Red Mountain.

been cemented by the ages). A six-foot ladder climbs over a stone wall, and suddenly you're engulfed in an arena of gnawed spires, twisted pillars, and hard-edged badlands. The reds of Red Mountain are not the saucy, seductive hues of Sedona or Monument Valley. They're more earthy tones, leaning in an orangish direction.

The inner basin spreads out among clustered hoodoos that beg for a little exploration. The surface makes for great grippy bouldering. It's like a hobbit-sized Bryce Canyon, vivid and endlessly entertaining. So yank the kids out of the ball pit at McDonald's and let them discover a natural playground.

Fast Fact: There are several versions of how Flagstaff acquired its name but all revolve around pioneer days when a lofty ponderosa pine was turned into a flagpole, visible for miles.

Where: From Flagstaff, drive northwest on Highway 180 for 25 miles. At milepost 247, turn left at the Forest Service sign marked "Red Mountain Geological Area." Take the dirt road a quarter mile to parking area.

Cost: Free. **Difficulty:** Easy.

Length: 3 miles round-trip.

Details: (928) 526-0866, www.fs.usda.gov/coconino.

THE LAND UNKNOWN Volcanoes are one of the all-time great movie props. If you're a fan of 1950s sci-fi like me, you know that anytime a plane or chopper goes down in or near a volcano, the occupants will invariably discover a tropical land teeming with dinosaurs. Volcanoes act as portals to mysterious lost worlds where the big thunder lizards bask in the heat of that boiling fury.

One of my favorites in the volcano/dinosaur sub-genre is *The Land Unknown* from 1957. It stars the always Tarzan-esque Jock Mahoney, a couple of monitor lizards, and a lumbering guy in a T-Rex suit who looks like Barney the Dinosaur's drunk uncle, the one who spoils Thanksgiving each year by passing out in the green bean casserole.

Miz Zip's FLAGSTAFF

Miz Zip's is a low-slung building tucked among a hodgepodge of businesses east from downtown. The cafe has been around since 1952. Before that it was Trixie's Diner, a juke joint with a rowdy reputation. The garish sign snags you. Miz Zip's, it announces in bold green letters, along with a Route 66 symbol and drawings of brawny burgers and thick-cut steaks. Two words are spelled out in neon, "Let's Eat." Heck yes, I always think, let's.

Slide into a booth or grab a stool at the horseshoe counter. Check out the chalkboard by the door for specials and pie selections. For lunch, choose from sandwiches aplenty including B.L.T.s, turkey melts, clubs, ham with eggs, or ham with cheese. But my heart belongs to the king of sandwiches, the burger. They butcher their own beef so quality is assured. No surprise, the Zipburger is a delight, like steak in casual clothes. Although—and this is where Miz Zip's and I part company—it's served with Thousand Island dressing. What is it with these joints that slather burgers with salad dressing? This is heresy. I order mine sans sauce and everything is jake. 2924 E. Route 66, (928) 526-0104.

"Anybody who doesn't think that the best hamburger place in the world is in his hometown is a sissy."

— CALVIN TRILLIN

Along the Way...

WATCH FOR ELK

Keep your eyes peeled when hiking Arizona's high country. Herds of elk roam the endless forests. Keep your ears open, too, because elk are a gabby bunch of ungulates. They're quick to vocalize warnings and identify one another by sounds. During the autumn mating season, bull elks bugle—a freakish and eerie call that splits the chilled air. It can start as a chesty bellow, escalating to a high-pitched squeal before winding down to a series of mumbled grunts. The first time I heard it, I thought a cougar with whooping cough had gotten its tail stuck in a blender.

HOORAY FOR HOLLYWOOD

Flagstaff very nearly became Tinsel Town. In 1913, pioneer filmmakers Cecil B. DeMille and Jesse Lasky were looking for a western location to shoot *The Squaw Man.* They hopped a train bound for Flagstaff but when they arrived, DeMille didn't approve of the snowy weather and high, mountainous terrain. They pushed on to the end of the line where they rented a barn in a sleepy burg called Hollywood. *The Squaw Man* proved to be so successful it helped launch the motion picture industry and established Hollywood as the movie capital of the world.

ASPENS

Aspens have tall trunks with smooth pale bark. They tend to grow at high elevations across Arizona in thick clusters, often with hundreds or even thousands of trees joined underground by a single root network. The leaves of aspen trees sharing root systems turn at the same time in autumn, creating a brilliant singular display of color.

Stands of quaking aspens may consist of a single clone or represent a mosaic of different clones. And they have a relationship with the wind unlike other trees. Aspens give voice to the slightest breeze. More than a forest, aspens are a symphony. Their leaves clatter happily, creating a velvet crescendo, a shimmery celebration. I always think it's the sound your heart makes when you accidentally run into an ex-lover on a day when you just happen to look fantastic.

RIORDAN MANSION

Flagstaff's Riordan Mansion is a sprawling two-family home built in 1904 and preserved as a window into Arizona's frontier past. Lumber baron brothers Michael and Timothy Riordan and their families somehow squeezed into the 13,000-square-foot 40-room mansion. This classic example of the Arts and Crafts style of architecture was designed by Charles Whittlesey, who also built El Tovar Hotel at Grand Canyon. Furnishings include priceless handcrafted tables and chairs by Gustav Stickley. Now operated as a state park, guided tours of the log and stone manse are offered daily. 409 W. Riordan Rd., (928) 779-4395, www.azstateparks.com.

Ferns for a carpet and aspens for a roof on Veit Springs Trail.

NO 4 Veit Springs Loop

Veit Springs is my oldest Arizona friend. It's the first trail I ever hiked in the state. As a freshman at NAU, I was on my way to English class one exquisite October morning when I glanced toward the San Francisco Peaks banded with yellow. Suddenly, nothing else mattered. Not Twain, not Faulkner, not even Kerouac. The aspens had turned.

I rounded up two like-minded scofflaws and we headed for Veit Springs, a short loop curling through lavish groves of the white-trunked trees and their vibrant canopy of heart-shaped leaves. Past a historic cabin and gurgling springs, at the foot of a basalt cliff adorned with pictographs, sits a field of sprawl-friendly boulders. For the rest of the afternoon, we lay draped atop the rocks like we

Hot Tip Opened in 1938, Arizona Snowbowl is one of the oldest continually operated ski areas in the country. During summertime they crank up the chair lift, whisking guests through the treetops to the upper slopes of Agassiz Peak at 11,500 feet for some stupendous views. The scenic sky ride operates from Memorial Day through mid-October. (928) 779-1951, www.arizonasnowbowl.com.

AUTUMN'S DIRTY SECRET It's weird that my strongest memory of Veit Springs is distinctly autumn-flavored, yet I almost never hike it then. I usually go in late spring when tender grass greens the meadows and acres of ferns unfurl small feathery fists. Dazzling though autumn might be, it's also fraught with melancholy...the whole back-to-school sense of impending doom that still grips me.

The older I get, the more I feud with winter. I hate the cold and I hate shrunken, shriveled days. Autumn is a winter enabler, tamping down temperatures and shaving off minutes of daylight. Suddenly there's a frost, then a freeze, then Santa Claus barges in and gobbles a plate of cookies. And none of it would be possible without autumn laying the groundwork. Ponder this: Autumn is the only season that uses an alias. Half the time it goes by its street name, Fall. That tells you the season has been mixed up in some ugly stuff in the past and can't be trusted.

A springhouse shelters the Veit Springs water source.

great kid-friendly hike with easy walking and plenty of nooks and crannies. Follow the cliff around to the left to discover a few red-orange pictographs, estimated to be more than a thousand years old.

Just below the rock art, a collection of big, comfortable boulders are spread among the aspens. Hooky recliners, I call them. If you see a middle-aged guy with a loopy grin stretched out atop a rock, pay him no mind. He might be a travel writer hard at work.

Where: From Flagstaff, drive north on U.S. 180 to Snowbowl Road and turn right. Travel 4.4 miles and watch for a small parking area on the right.

Cost: Free. **Difficulty:** Easy.

Length: 1.5-mile loop.

Details: (928) 774-5045, www.azgfd.gov.

Fast Fact: Pictographs are images painted on rocks, not to be confused with petroglyphs, which are created by carving or incising part of a rock surface. Pictographs are much rarer.

had been poured there. Shafts of sunlight streamed through the rustling patchwork of lemon and saffron above us, and every breeze triggered the soft fireworks of fluttering golden leaves.

The trail begins as a gentle climb along an old Jeep road to a small preserve. This 160-acre tract was homesteaded in 1892 by Ludwig Veit. It's now managed by the Arizona Game and Fish Department and is known as the Lamar Haines Memorial Wildlife Area. Elk and deer are common sights mornings and evenings. The road soon narrows to a path and reaches a fork at 0.2 miles. Take the loop clockwise.

Just before reaching a plaque honoring Haines, a Flagstaff educator and environmentalist, a spur trail leads to the tumbledown remains of Veit's cabin and two small springhouses. Veit Springs makes a

Mysterious pictographs adorn cliffs above Veit Springs.

 Satchmo's FLAGSTAFF

The luckiest customers at Satchmo's are the ones when owner Jamie Thousand works the kitchen, because he's always whipping up something new and then bringing it around for folks to try. That's how I first sampled burnt ends. Nuggets are whittled off the points of a brisket. The small chunks are cooked quickly on the flattop just to crust them, and served on white bread. They are a sweet, crunchy, smoky delicacy that I gobbled like beef candy.

If you know barbecue, you'll recognize burnt ends as a Kansas City signature. Thousand grew up near Hannibal, Missouri, and brings plenty of KC passion to his restaurant. The Cajun items on the menu stem from an extended stay in college when dining budgets had to be stretched.

Three smokers seem to be going all the time at Satchmo's. They use cherry, pecan, and hickory wood, depending on which meat is being transformed. While the barbecue is a standout, I find myself exploring the Cajun side of the menu more and more. The Catfish Po'Boy is an exquisitely balanced sandwich with waves of complementary flavors rolling across my taste buds. 1924 Arrowhead Avenue, (928) 774-7292, www.satchmosaz.com.

"If I could not walk far and fast,
I think I should just explode and perish."

— CHARLES DICKENS

TOP 5 REASONS TO TAKE UP HIKING

5. Every bag of Peanut M&Ms you buy qualifies as trail mix.

4. Helps fund the massive multinational hiking sock industry.

3. Everyone should spend some reflective time with their thoughts and venomous snakes.

2. Shedding unwanted pounds will help you look good in wedding gown/mall cop uniform/prison jumpsuit, depending on your future plans.

1. They don't call it the Great Indoors.

CHAPTER 2

SEDONA
⊱ AND THE ⊰
Verde Valley

NESTLED AT THE MOUTH OF Oak Creek Canyon and surrounded by a sea of red sandstone, Sedona exists at an impossible intersection: a real-life getaway and fantasyland escape. It's a dream town, the primo one in Arizona. There's a siren song to this place. Folks vacation in Sedona—hiking, biking, and meditating among giant sculpted formations. Cares melt away and suddenly they're cruising residential neighborhoods with a realtor.

As a Verde Valley resident, I say forget about moving here. It's not the utopia you imagine. You have to put up with views cluttered by red rock drama, relentless sunshine, and me always dropping by to borrow a cup of pickles.

№5 Hangover Trail, Sedona

For a town that's lousy with sandstone, Sedona remains downright miserly regarding the slickrock experience. Several trails cross patches of exposed stone, buffed smooth by rain and wind, but not in a large expanse like southern Utah's canyon country. There's no hiking I like better. Hoofing across the slant and slope of petrified waves is like walking on the bones of the land. If you want slickrock hiking around these parts, head

~~~~~~~~

Left: The joyful skyscrapers of Sedona are unmistakable.

for Hangover.

The Hangover is a bewitching clamber up a long spine of red stone with devastating views every step. Start on Cow Pies Trail, an easy path cutting through scrubby woodlands. Where Cow Pies branches off, continue toward Mitten Ridge.

I'm reminded of the Fred Astaire movie, *Royal Wedding*, where he's dancing like mad, then taps his way up the walls and onto the ceiling. I'm walking through forest toward a cliff of sandstone, then boom! I'm walking up the wall.

This is the magic of slickrock hiking, requiring good grippy soles and a little faith. I pursue a curving route marked by painted white hexagons. I flow across the contours of rock, toward a large saddle separating the Bear Wallow and Oak Creek drainages.

Hangover started as a mountain bike trail and was officially adopted by the forest service in 2012. I'm not a mountain biker, but many friends are. Good people, but honestly I think they're

Fast Fact: The town of Sedona was named by its first postmaster, T. C. Schnebly. His original suggestions of Oak Creek Crossing and Schnebly's Station were rejected by the Postmaster General in Washington as too long. So T. C. simply named the community after his lovely wife, Sedona.

Scary for mountain bikers, Hangover is a delight for hikers.

Cowboy Club　SEDONA

nuttier than an elephant burp. And hiking this trail does nothing to change my opinion. Ideal for bipeds, it must be terrifying from a bike seat with steep plunges down exposed rock. Hangover is rated double black diamond (akin to a big skull and crossbones) and should only be attempted by experienced, slightly unhinged bikers.

As I cross the saddle and begin a sharp traverse down the cliff face, I'm recalibrating my Top Five Sedona hikes to include this beauty. First time in my life I'm in love with a hangover. I drop into a nifty little bowl, and then latch onto a thin ribbon of a path clinging to the slope as it passes beneath a protrusion of overhanging rock. This section prompted the trail name. From here I'm treated to sensational views of Midgley Bridge swarming with ant-sized tourists.

I cross one final saddle and ease down the ridge toward the trailhead.

Where: From the "Y" intersection of Arizona 179 and Arizona 89A, take 179 south 0.3 miles. Turn left on Schnebly Hill Road and drive 3.5 miles to a signed parking area. The last 2.5 miles is a rugged dirt road requiring a high clearance vehicle.

Cost: Free. **Difficulty:** Moderate.

Length: 4.3 miles round-trip.

Details: (928) 203-2900, www.redrockcountry.org.

This is a hunk of history sitting in Uptown Sedona. The Cowboy Club used to be Oak Creek Tavern, a popular watering hole. During the heyday of movie filming in Sedona, this was the hangout for Hollywood's A-list. Locals had the chance to bend the casual elbow with the likes of John Wayne, Burt Lancaster, Robert Mitchum, and Jimmy Stewart. In 1965, a group of pards who split their time between the saddle and the studio formed Cowboy Artists of America over cold beers in the tavern.

Now a slightly upscale restaurant with an eclectic menu, the Cowboy Club isn't your typical burger joint. Snag a table on the patio for the great views and for the gleeful sensation of having lunch outdoors in beautiful Arizona. Burgers are a fresh ground chuck and sirloin blend, nicely executed. A buttery, yet surprisingly sturdy, pretzel bun holds the meat and toppings together, absorbing the juices for the few fleeting seconds it takes me to devour the beast. 241 N. Arizona 89A, (928) 282-4200, www.cowboyclub.com.

"You can find your way across this country using burger joints the way a navigator uses stars."

— CHARLES KURALT

Along the Way...

COWBOY LIFE

If you're yearning for a cowboy experience, mosey over to M Diamond Ranch for a horseback ride into spaces so wide open, tumbleweeds have to cross the prairie in relay teams. The M Diamond was homesteaded in 1908 and has been a working cattle ranch ever since. It offers the only rides permitted by the Red Rock Ranger District of the Coconino National Forest. There are two wilderness areas and several major archaeological sites near ranch headquarters. Besides the guided trail rides, the ranch offers cowboy cookouts with entertainment. (928) 300-6466, www.sedonahorsebackrides.com.

VORTEXES

Even if you're not an adherent of the New Age movement, visit one of Sedona's famous vortexes. Because here's the wonderful secret: Vortexes are located at some of the most scenic spots among the red rocks. What is a vortex? Sedona vortexes (the proper grammatical form "vortices" is rarely used) are thought to be swirling centers of energy conducive to spiritual healing, meditation, and self-exploration. Believers identify four primary vortexes: Boynton Canyon, Bell Rock, Cathedral Rock, and Airport Mesa. Find out more from Sedona Metaphysical Spiritual Association: (928) 300-7796, www.sedonaspiritual.com.

SCHNEBLY HILL ROAD

Driving to the Hangover trailhead, Schnebly Hill Road is a bouncy, teeth-rattling ride. The rugged wagon route was scratched from flinty slopes by Sedona pioneers at the turn of the last century. You've navigated the toughest section by the time you reach the trail. For great views, continue a few miles farther as it makes a twisted ascent through red rock tablelands to the pine forests of the Colorado Plateau.

After the first paved mile, the road turns primitive, a lane pock-marked and ledged. It's probably best not to tackle Schnebly Hill in a sedan unless you have no affection for your oil pan. Although Lisa Schnebly Heidinger, a fine Arizona author and great-granddaughter of T. C. and Sedona Schnebly, told me that whenever her father gets a new convertible, he "baptizes" it by driving the road.

If you don't have high clearance (or if your family name isn't on the street sign) consider taking a Jeep tour. A steady stream of Sedona's commercial Jeep companies snake their way up Schnebly Hill daily.

Left: A steady climb and swooping descent add spice to Hiline.
Opposite: Hiline Trail drops Cathedral Rock right in your lap.

N⁰ 6 Hiline Trail, Sedona

The Hiline shares similar parentage as the Hangover. It is another stunning trail with outlandish panoramas built by bikers and adopted by the forest service in 2012. This also earned a double black diamond rating for spoke-jockeys. Hiline, Hangover, and their ilk are turning Sedona into a primo mountain-biking destination similar to Moab, Utah.

From the trailhead at Yavapai Vista, a knot of short connector trails branches off, but maps are posted at each junction. Follow Kaibab Trail to Slim Shady to Hiline. And I can't be sure, but I think Slim Shady is the only Sedona trail that shares an alter ego moniker with a rapper (Eminem).

Hiline wiggles up a narrow gulley to a rocky slope and then tilts upward, an eyebrow of a trail pasted against the tall promontory known as the Pedestal. The climb is steady, but I never notice because I'm stopping every few feet to close my gaping jaw. Lavish views of multiple formations include Bell Rock, Courthouse Butte, and Cathedral Rock, beautifully framed by swatches of forest.

Make the mesa top your picnic/turnaround spot if you don't want to do the full seven miles. The trail tumbles off the backside, dropping in a series of red rock ledges providing various angles of Cathedral along the way. Keep an eye peeled for bikers hurtling through here. Over bare rock, just follow the dabs of white paint.

The trail continues to descend a few hundred yards before leveling off and entering a dry streambed flanked by sun-dappled woodlands. Hiline junctions with the Baldwin Trail after 3.5 miles. If you've come this far, there's no need to hurry right back. I hang a right on Baldwin and a half-mile later I'm under a dense canopy of cottonwood and sycamores, on the edge of silver-tongued Oak Creek. This is a Tom Sawyer–quality hooky spot, perfect for fishing or snoozing the afternoon away. I choose the latter.

Where: From the "Y" intersection of Arizona 179 and Arizona 89A, take 179 south 5.5 miles to Yavapai Vista Trailhead. Yavapai Vista can only be accessed via southbound Arizona 179.

Cost: A Red Rock Pass is required—$5 per day—and is available at the trailhead kiosk.

Difficulty: Moderate. **Length:** 7 miles round-trip.
Details: (928) 203-2900, www.redrockcountry.org.

Hot Tip Sedona was meant to be viewed from a helicopter. Drop in and out of backcountry gorges, buzz through corridors of vertical stone, and glide along sharp-edged ridgelines with vistas splashing through the windows. Arizona Helicopter Adventures: (800) 282-5141, www.azheli.com. Sedona Air Tours: (888) 866-7433, www.sedonaairtours.com.

PJ's Village Pub & Sports Lounge

Never trust a bar without a jukebox. A bar with no jukebox is a nightclub or possibly a library. And the tune cabinet at PJ's is a dandy. Seems like every time I'm there it blasts out an unexpected song that whisks me back to my wide-eyed, loose-moraled youth.

PJ's is an old-school sports bar. It's a saloon first and foremost with a long bar, concrete floor, and exposed rafters. Walls are adorned with sports memorabilia, neon signs, and several strategically mounted televisions. There's plenty of bar food to be had, but burgers rule. Each patty is one-third pound of certified Angus beef and served on a brioche bun. Their signature burger is the Boomer, topped with American and Swiss cheeses and grilled pastrami. 40 West Cortez Drive, (928) 284-2250, www.pjsvillagepub.com.

NO 7 Marg's Draw, Sedona

Some people play hooky, but not me. I take hooky very seriously.

Certain days demand you slip free from small responsibilities. Days like this—on the cusp of spring, balmy enough for shorts, with a sky belligerently blue. I couldn't stay at the computer a minute longer as March tapped on the window with soft primrose knuckles. I'm only flesh and blood.

Marg's Draw, named for a mule owned by one of the area's first pioneers, makes the perfect hooky trail. Marg, the mule, used to hide out in this scenic area to avoid work. To celebrate that irrepressible spirit, I follow in Marg's hoofsteps.

The trail starts from the parking lot at the end of the pavement on Schnebly Hill Road. Marg's Draw crosses the road and disappears into the woods. This easy hike carves out a path through the

Snoopy Rock snoozes above Marg's Draw.

Marg the mule may have admired the panoramas surrounding her hideout.

Munds Mountain Wilderness, skirting the Copper Cliffs and Snoopy Rock, one of the town's most prominent formations. Plenty of Sedona's rocks are easy to recognize, others not so much. Lots of names have been around forever while some like Snoopy and Spaceship are more recent additions.

Of all Sedona formations, I think Coffee Pot is the most obvious. It has that, "Oh yeah, I see it!" factor. Yet what happens when the memory of old-time coffee pots fades? Are name changes on the horizon? Will we soon be hiking Keurig Rock and iPad Point?

The path crosses the draw at a lovely, dry waterfall and ends at Broken Arrow trailhead, providing additional hiking possibilities. Much of the route lies a mere crystal's throw from civilization, yet the dense screen of vegetation provides a genuine backcountry experience. Instant access to hidden wonders is one of Sedona's many charms. Marg would approve.

Where: From the "Y" intersection of Arizona 179 and Arizona 89A, take 179 south 0.3 miles. Turn left on Schnebly Hill Road and drive 1 mile to a signed parking area.

Cost: A Red Rock Pass is required—$5 per day—and is available at the trailhead kiosk.

Difficulty: Easy.

Length: 4 miles round-trip.

Details: (928) 203-2900, www.redrockcountry.org.

Sandstone cliffs and boulders along Marg's Draw Trail.

Simon's Hot Dogs SEDONA

Simon's occupies a closet-sized space just inside the front door of Oak Creek Brewing Company. So on your way to or from a frosty beverage, you catch the aroma of smoky franks. It is a killer marketing plan. The signature dog is the Colombian. The all-beef wiener is tucked into a soft, wide bun, crowded with mozzarella cheese, crushed potato chips, chunks of pineapple, and topped with a creamy sauce. It's one of those curious hot dog–only combinations that somehow works. The pineapple adds the

right note of sweetness to the saltier ingredients.

The Cowboy comes topped with homemade chili and mozzarella cheese, while the Hola Amigo nestles with avocado, cream cheese, and jalapenos. The latest addition is the Tokyo, piled with teriyaki onions, wasabi mayo, and nori, seaweed loaded with nutritional benefits.

Anytime you can sit in a bar eating a hot dog as part of a health regimen, that's an opportunity that shouldn't be missed. 2050 Yavapai Drive, (928) 496-0266, www.simon-hot-dogs.com.

N<u>o</u> 8   West Fork Trail, Sedona

This creekside walk into a high-walled, forested gorge is considered by many to be Arizona's most beautiful hike. And in a state with the Grand Canyon, that says plenty. In the spring of 2014 when the Slide Fire swept through the canyon, West Fork was spared serious harm thanks to the heroic efforts of firefighters. The trail was singed in spots at ground level but remains gorgeous.

The Call of the Canyon Day-Use Area features restrooms and picnic tables. A paved path leads past informational signs to an arched footbridge. After crossing the bridge, the trail reverts to dirt and rambles through an old orchard where aged trees still bend under the weight of their fruit. Beyond the orchard, the ruins of Mayhew Lodge are tucked among the brush.

From here, the path traces a gentle stream into a narrow defile between soaring cliffs. It's a mesmerizing combination of soft forest and sheer stone, intimacy and dizzying drama. The maintained trail is about three miles and includes a dozen creek crossings, so a sturdy walking stick makes a welcome companion.

This was a trail I hiked often, back when it was less accessible. No signs and no parking kept

most folks away. I have an allergy to crowds and gravitate toward trails that fly under the radar. Yet I stopped by early one summer morning to revisit West Fork, and it felt like I had come home.

Echoes of birdsong and the splashy stream fill the canyon. The trail parallels the meandering creek the whole way. Crossings generally involve a short hop over strategically positioned rocks, so wear shoes you don't mind getting wet. And be sure you know how to identify poison ivy—"Leaves of three, let them be"— because it is plentiful along the water, growing among the grapevines, sumac, and Virginia creeper.

> **Fast Fact:** While staying in the cabins at the head of West Fork, which would become Mayhew Lodge, western writer Zane Grey penned the words to *The Call of the Canyon*. It was the first of his novels snapped up by Hollywood. At Grey's insistence, the filmmakers shot the 1923 silent movie on location.

The erosion-scarred sandstone creates unique ledges and overhangs that kids (and middle-aged mugs like me) love. I found one of my favorite spots here, a big waterside boulder where I sat for a long while, just letting the soft morning brush past me.

Around three miles in, sheer canyon walls close

Autumn turns West Fork into a colorful jungle.

Canyon walls soar above the lush forest cradling West Fork.

around you. The maintained portion of the trail ends soon afterward at an expansive pool lapping at brutish cliffs. This is the normal turnaround spot.

Hot Tip Every first Friday of the month, Sedona's prominent art galleries host an evening of openings, demonstrations, and receptions. First Friday Art Walk takes place from 5–8 p.m., www.sedonagalleryassociation.com.

I was happy to see my old friend again. The canyon was quiet in the early morning. I met plenty of folks on my return hike, lots of voices and laughter interrupting my solitude. But I was okay with that. I guess a little time beside a gentle stream can soften the heart of even a cantankerous curmudgeon.

Where: Trailhead is at Call of the Canyon Day-Use Area, 9.5 miles north of Sedona on Arizona 89A.

Cost: $10 per vehicle or $2 walk-ins. Red Rock Pass is not accepted here.

Difficulty: Easy. **Length:** 6.4 miles round-trip.

Details: (928) 203-2900, www.redrockcountry.org.

"I'm not telling you, 'Never eat a hamburger.' Just eat the good ones with real beef, you know, like the ones from the mom-and-pop diner down the street...and it's so good that when you take a bite out of that burger, you just know somewhere in the world a vegan is crying."

—HOMER SIMPSON

Garland's Indian Gardens Café & Market

SEDONA

This is the country market all country markets aspire to become. Eclectic, historic, and tucked in the scenic heart of Oak Creek Canyon, it seems more oasis than store. Recent renovations have expanded the seating area inside, including a stand-up bar for wine tasting. They also stock more than one hundred bottled beers to quench that post-hike thirst. The menu emphasizes locally grown and organic products.

Hearty, creative sandwiches go well beyond standard lunchmeat and cheese duets. The Ferrari comes with prosciutto, fresh mozzarella, roasted red pepper, tomato, onion, basil, and vinaigrette on a baguette. It's like a caprese salad in sandwich form. Be sure to grab a bag of organic apples grown right in Oak Creek Canyon and a jug of cider. And while the seating inside is nice, don't miss the tree-swaddled patio in back. 3951 N. Arizona 89A, (928) 282-7702, www.indiangardens.com.

HIKE HOUSE One of your first stops in Sedona should be the Hike House, an all-in-one facility for serious outdoorsy types. Their Sedona Trail Finder is a high-definition, interactive technology that steers you toward one of the 100+ area trails based on your ability and desire. You'll find footwear, apparel, and gear in the upscale store. The Energy Cafe whips up homemade wraps, sandwiches, and fresh-baked cookies to eat at a patio table or stuff into your daypack. They also have a trail mix station where you can make your own. Every Tuesday morning they offer a free guided hike and hiking clinic, providing practical tips for Sedona trails. 431 Arizona 179, (928) 282-5820, www.thehikehouse.com.

NO 9 Parsons Trail, Clarkdale

I'll come right out and say it—this trail is all kinds of spectacular, dropping from scrubby high desert into a jungle-like oasis that goes for miles. Imagine the towering red buttes of Oak Creek Canyon but with no roads or resorts, no homes or hotels. You've just conjured up an image of adjacent Sycamore Canyon. Parsons Trail provides the easiest access to this rugged wilderness area.

A sweet, sweet swimming hole on Parsons Trail.

At the beginning, the trail scrambles 200 feet down the canyon wall to the creek bed. From there it's easygoing through a virtual tunnel of leafy shade alongside Sycamore Creek. Fed by several springs, pools form all along the way, rippled mirrors reflecting the lush canopy of treetops and high cliffs that surround you.

The trail is generally easy to follow, swinging from one side of the stream to the other about a half dozen times. Sometimes I'm walking through sand, other times I'm crossing stone ledges at the water's edge. Flash floods occasionally roar through to realign the route, but keep your eyes peeled and you should have no problem finding your way. Just remember to never stray far from the creek.

During spring a riot of wildflowers erupt, and in summer months the largest pools turn into excellent swimming holes featuring grand diving ledges. At about four miles you reach Parsons Spring, a wide marshy area. This marks the end of the trail and the end of reliable water in Sycamore Canyon. The rest of the vast canyon is a fiercely scenic but arid wilderness.

Where: From Cottonwood, drive northwest on Main Street, following signs to Tuzigoot National Monument. Turn right on Tuzigoot Road, cross the Verde River, and turn left on Sycamore Canyon Road (FR 131). Drive about 11 miles to the trailhead. The dirt road has a couple of rough spots but is usually accessible to sedans.

Cost: Free. **Difficulty:** Easy.
Length: 8 miles round-trip.
Details: (928) 203-2900, www.redrockcountry.org.

Haunted Hamburger
JEROME

Going to Jerome and not eating on the deck of the Haunted Hamburger is like going to the Grand Canyon and never looking down. They have a complete menu but anyone who can saunter into a place called Haunted Hamburger and *not* order a burger possesses either an abundance of willpower or a lack of common sense.

This former boardinghouse clings to the side of the mountain, like just about everything in Jerome. There's a cozy dining room with a big picture window, but grab a seat on the covered deck if you can. Views roll across the Verde Valley to the red cliffs of Sedona and the San Francisco Peaks beyond. Expect a generous slab of beef cradled on a cushiony bun baked fresh on the premises. Inside, they provide a full topping bar so you can heap on the fixings. The trusting fools. My creations always soar so high I need Sherpas to hoist the final pickles. 410 N. Clark Street, (928) 634-0554, www.thehauntedhamburger.com.

This refreshing summer moment brought to you by Parsons Trail.

Along the Way...

SEDONA HERITAGE MUSEUM

The focus of Sedona Heritage Museum is split between exhibits on apple growing, cowboys, and movies. That trifecta is rarely seen in museums but it neatly sums up Sedona's history. This was cowboy country, but early settlers thrived along Oak Creek by growing apples and peaches. And nearly 100 feature films were shot in Sedona, so the movie room features photo stills, posters, storyboards, a diorama of the old western movie set, and a loop of Sedona-based flicks. The setting, a peaceful homestead and orchard in Jordan Historical Park, is worth a visit alone. 735 Jordan Road, (928) 282-7038, www.sedonamuseum.org.

THE JOY OF HOOKY

I call myself a travel writer but that's sugarcoating the truth. What I am in reality is a professional bad influence. Everything I write is to encourage you to play hooky. Call in sick and go for a hike. Skip out of that afternoon meeting and go for a bike ride. Ignore those weekend chores and take a road trip.

   I am a firm believer in the power of hooky. The small rebellion of hooky keeps us from being overwhelmed and maintains balance in our lives. Slipping beyond the clawing grasp of minor obligations to seize a bite-sized morsel of freedom reconnects us to that rakish, devil-may-care person we always planned to become. When responsibility locks down our spirit, occasional forays of hooky keeps the door ajar.

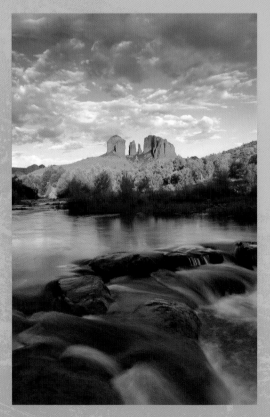

SUNSET VIEWS

Late afternoon seems to trigger a mass exodus from Sedona. As if by signal, a stream of traffic heads for the airport. Yet folks aren't rushing to catch a flight out of town. They're angling for high ground. Sedona's airport straddles a long mesa, and on this elevated perch crowds assemble to witness a red rock sunset. While sunsets from Airport Mesa are spectacular, they're also crowded. Here are options for a quieter experience:

   1. Visit Crescent Moon Picnic Area, known as Red Rock Crossing, and watch the fading light melt down the sides of Cathedral Rock like warm honey.

   2. Make the short hike up the backside of Sugarloaf in West Sedona. Barely a nub of a hill and surrounded by more imposing cliffs, Sugarloaf hardly seems worth the effort, but trust me, it's fantástico.

   3. The Girdner Trail is located at the end of Cultural Park Place. Enjoy great views from the upper reaches of the path or picnic tables at the trailhead.

Fast Fact: When *USA Weekend* compiled their Most Beautiful Places in America list, Sedona claimed the top spot.

WELCOME TO JEROME Clinging to the steep slope of Mingus Mountain, Jerome teeters over a mile in the air overlooking the Verde Valley. The vertical burg established boomtown credentials when copper mines churned out a billion dollars of ore. In the 1920s some 15,000 toe-clenched residents sneered at gravity long enough to call Jerome their home.

World War II marked the last copper boomlet as Jerome fell into disrepair. Mines closed in 1953 and citizens scattered—all except a few dozen hearty, ornery souls who formed a historical society and began patching the scars and knitting the bones of the tumbledown town. In the 1960s Jerome experienced a counterculture renaissance—a polite way of saying hippies moved in. They snapped up cheap real estate, opened shops, restaurants, art galleries, and, most important, injected Jerome with the relaxed, carefree vibe still prevalent.

VERDE CANYON RAILROAD The casual grace of riding the rails never goes out of style. The more hurried our lives and the more bullied we are by technology, the more we long for moments of simplicity and wonder.

The Verde Canyon Railroad is an excursion train departing from Clarkdale. It makes a forty-mile round-trip into the remote wilderness of Verde Canyon, nestled between two national forests at the confluence of desert and wetland. Vintage diesel locomotives power the train through a lush riparian corridor carved by the Verde River, the water canopied by cottonwoods as sunlight careens diamond-like from the surface. High sandstone cliffs rise overhead and provide winter home to a large population of bald and golden eagles. The train travels along a section of standard gauge track built in 1911 to support the mining in Jerome. First class and coach accommodations are available and all cars provide access to open-air viewing platforms, which is where you'll spend most of your time. (800) 293-7245, www.verdecanyonrr.com.

NO 10 Thumper Loop, Cottonwood

While it may not be as dazzling as trails at Grand Canyon or even nearby Sedona, this is my home field. Located just minutes from my house, I have logged more miles on the dirt paths in Dead Horse Ranch State Park than anywhere else in Arizona.

Perched on the Verde River and sheltering a rare cottonwood and willow riparian forest, Dead Horse is a crown jewel in the state park system. The Thumper Loop consists of three trails: Lower Raptor, Thumper, and Lime Kiln. And I hike one portion or another weekly. The trail is always there for me. It soothes me during hard times, celebrates my victories, gives me a quiet place to think, entertains me, inspires me, keeps me healthy, and most of all, vanishes me. That's the magic of a trail.

> **Hot Tip** In recent years, Cottonwood has grown into a destination for wine lovers with boutique vineyards huddled on sloping volcanic hills and several tasting rooms located in Old Town, the historic heart of Cottonwood. www.vvwinetrail.com.

Mountain bikers tackle the loop clockwise from the Lower Raptor trailhead. I prefer to start at Lime Kiln with parking at the lagoons, which bustle with activity. Ducks drift across the water, redwing blackbirds chatter in the cattails, and gangly great blue herons stand on the shore, all legs and curious necks, preening like it's prom night. From November through March, the lagoons are stocked with trout, luring bald eagles that winter on the Verde River.

The trail traces a limestone ridge past the remains of an old kiln. After a short, steep climb known as the Stairs, the route levels off and slices through hills, dotted with junipers, pines, and bowed crucifixion thorns. Big sky and sweet views all the way. After a couple of miles, hang a left onto Thumper. This is a lovely segment, rambling across rolling plateaus, dipping in and out of shallow canyons.

After 2.25 miles on Thumper, turn left on Lower Raptor. You begin a gradual descent dropping

A rickety cabin and ruins of Tuzigoot visible from Thumper Loop.

Fast Fact: In the late 1940s, the Ireys family looked at ranches in Cottonwood, including one with the bleached bones of a deceased equine. When the father asked which ranch they liked, the kids said "the one with the dead horse." In 1973 when they sold the property to Arizona State Parks, the Ireys made retaining the name a condition of the sale.

via terraced ridges. Along the way you're treated to sprawling views of Cottonwood, Clarkdale, Jerome, and the ruins of Tuzigoot National Monument, a prehistoric pueblo site perched dramatically above a bend in the Verde River. The trail ends at a campground and a series of pathways leads back to the lagoons where your vehicle is parked. The loop is 7.2 miles but you'll total about 8 by the time you reach your ride.

Where: From Cottonwood, drive northwest on Main Street, following the signs to Dead Horse Ranch State Park.

Cost: $7 per vehicle.

Difficulty: Moderate.

Length: 8 miles.

Details: (928) 634-5283, www.azstateparks.com.

WILDLIFE APLENTY I've seen wildlife aplenty during my years of hiking. One of my favorite sightings was during a morning hike on Lower Raptor. Suddenly a jackrabbit exploded over the top of a small hill running flat out with a coyote hot on his heels. The jack sprinted right toward me—either by design or happy accident—then zoomed past as I stood motionless. Suddenly, the coyote spotted me and swerved away at the last second. To put it in basketball parlance, I set a pick for a jackrabbit.

If it had been a roadrunner being chased by a coyote—especially a coyote wearing rocket-powered roller skates from the Acme Corporation—it would have been the greatest day of my life.

"May your trails be crooked, winding, lonesome, dangerous, leading to the most amazing view."

— EDWARD ABBEY

Verde Lea Market Deli & Grill COTTONWOOD

I love grocery store burgers. Maybe it's a southern thing but it seemed like every little country market I visited in Kentucky and Tennessee had hamburgers sizzling behind the deli counter. These rural outposts had to supply many needs, and those hand-formed burgers still haunt my dreams. Verde Lea Market, a neighborhood grocery, maintains that tradition and feeds work crews from all over the Verde Valley.

The burgers are grilled masterpieces of fresh ground chuck. Buns are baked daily. The Frisco comes laden with cheddar and green chile on a sourdough bun. The Crown, topped with tangy pastrami, snaps your head back at first bite. But by far the most popular item is not a burger but the burly sandwich known as a torta. Owner Bill Murray credits his torta with keeping the business afloat during the first lean years. It starts with telera bread for a

hint of sweetness, followed by a thin layer of beans, a heaping portion of carne asada, grilled onions, lettuce, tomato, and a fistful of jalapenos to create a savory jaw-unhinging sandwich that customers call addictive. 516 N. Main Street., (928) 634-8731, www.verdelea.com.

OUT OF AFRICA WILDLIFE PARK

Nestled in the high desert of Camp Verde, just minutes from Cottonwood, Out of Africa Wildlife Park provides a comfortable sanctuary for 400 exotic animals, and features dozens of large predators. The preserve is spread across 104 acres of rolling terrain in the Black Hills, a setting that bears a striking resemblance to many regions of Africa. The sprawling, natural habitats eliminate much of the stress-induced behavior noticeable in animals held in captivity. The boredom of more traditional zoos seems nonexistent here.

Tiger Splash is the signature show of Out of Africa. There is no training and no tricks. The daily show is all spontaneous, just animals frolicking with their caretakers. Fierce tigers engage in the sort of activities every housecat owner will recognize. It's just the grand scale that makes it so impressive. (928) 567-2840, www.outofafricapark.com.

CENTRAL
Highlands

WHEN I PONDER Northern Arizona hiking destinations, I think of the sculpted sandstone of Sedona, big aspen groves of Flagstaff, and the gaping maw of Grand Canyon. I tend to overlook the central highlands—even Prescott because, you know, it's Prescott. Nice mountains but no knife-edged drama. And it's more about the courthouse than the canyons. I realize now that I've been a hiking snob.

In recent years, a dedicated army of volunteers has built a series of enticing pathways all over town. Loops, connectors, and out-and-backs have been added to a network of existing trails. Prescott has been transformed into a playground for bipeds. I'm quite happy to take advantage of that.

№11 Salida Gulch Trail, Prescott

I showed up on a Saturday afternoon expecting to encounter crowds on this bucolic loop through the woods above Lynx Creek. Instead, I had the trail to myself. Guess I'm not the only one overlooking Prescott. This is a good introductory hike because it showcases a wide sample of the area. It passes cacti, scrubby chaparral, willow and walnut trees, and climbs into ponderosa pines with sweet

The Granite Dells throw a stony embrace around Watson Lake.

mountain views.

The trail begins off Salida Connection. A stone's throw from the trailhead, you cross the creek and pass a gate. Immediately take the turnoff for Trail #95. That's Salida Gulch. Hang a left, taking the loop clockwise. The first leg traces a riparian strip in a peaceful canyon, cooled by the stream and patches of shade. Old gold mining operations left behind plenty of scars along this creek, but you'd never notice now after forest service restoration.

About a half-mile in, to the left of the trail you can see panels of intricate rock art carved into a cliff of stacked boulders. Renderings of animals, stylized human forms, and geometric shapes are spread across the stone face. Look but don't touch. The oils from your skin will degrade these artifacts over time.

Hot Tip Courthouse Plaza functions as an old-fashioned town square. Events take place on the stately lawn throughout the year and range from art shows to music festivals to holiday gatherings. www.visit-prescott.com.

I'm always fascinated by these links to a long-vanished civilization. What story do they tell? About two miles away, hundreds of people are in Costco buying Pop Tarts by the pallet. Meanwhile,

Into the soft pine forest of Salida Gulch. **Right:** Look at but don't touch the rock art along Salida Gulch Trail.

I'm gazing at ancient carvings and listening to a raven's wing slicing pine-scented air. Sometimes hiking is more than just walking.

A mile past the petroglyphs, the trail banks to the right and begins an easy climb up the ridge. It's such a gentle grade that it's barely noticeable. Before long I'm ambling along the ridgeline through a thin forest fattened by layers of chaparral. The trees break apart, exposing big vistas of rolling pine-clad mountains. Soon the trail drops back down to the gulch, rejoining Salida Connection.

Where: From downtown Prescott, head east on Arizona 69 to Walker Road. (If you reach Costco you just passed it.) Proceed 1.2 miles and turn left on Lynx Creek Road. Travel 0.9 miles to a large parking area on the right. Portions of the road are graded dirt, suitable for all vehicles.

Cost: Free. **Difficulty:** Easy.

Length: 4.2 miles round-trip.

Details: (928) 443-8000, www.fs.usda.gov/prescott.

Fast Facts: Founded in 1864, Prescott served as Arizona's first territorial capital.

— Doc Holliday's girlfriend, Big Nose Kate, died in Prescott in 1940 at the age of 89 and is buried in town.

Bill's Grill   PRESCOTT

I loved this joint as soon as I walked in. The place is like one big screened-in porch. Plastic tablecloths, sun streaming in, and a full menu of beers and burgers create a welcome atmosphere. Sure, there's a full bar inside with seating but you can't pry me away from a sunny window. I'm drawn to natural light. If I visit your home sometime and disappear for a few minutes, don't worry. I'm not upstairs rooting through your drawers; I'm simply on the veranda. I'll always be on the veranda. If you don't have a veranda, chances are I won't visit.

Burgers here are built from the foundation up. They grind their own beef daily and you pick your patty. Choose between Angus beef, hormone-free local beef, plain, blackened, onion-smashed, or fresh cracked black pepper. They offer several specialty burgers as well and a far-ranging topping menu (for a slight charge) that includes surprises like artichoke hearts and grilled eggplant. They also serve ten different sauces to slather on your creation from curried honey mustard to peanut butter, if you want to play mad scientist. I love the attention to detail. There are plenty of other sandwiches and vegetarian options, too, but someone else will have to tell you about them. I get the burger. 333 S. Montezuma Street, (928) 237-9138, www.billsgrillprescott.com.

Along the Way...

SHARLOT HALL MUSEUM

Sharlot Hall Museum gives visitors a chance to stroll through the past and even chat with it. The museum is built around the site of the First Territorial Governor's Mansion, with other historic buildings scattered across beautifully landscaped grounds. The living history program has staff and volunteers dressed in period garb, offering detailed accounts of Prescott's frontier days. Sharlot Hall was a poet, journalist, and historian and the first woman to hold public office in the territory. Her personal collection of artifacts served as the foundation to this extraordinary museum. 415 W. Gurley Street, (928) 445-3122, www.sharlot.org.

Hassayampa Inn

SPEND THE NIGHT

Spend the night in Prescott if possible. You'll find great lodging options. If you're into grand dame historic hotels, you can't do better than Hassayampa Inn. Designed by renowned architect, Henry Trost and opened in 1927, it hasn't changed much except for a few modern conveniences being added. The elegant lobby shows off the bone structure and graceful lines of her youth. 122 E. Gurley Street, (800) 322-1927, www.hassayampainn.com.

Stay at a place called The Motor Lodge and you know you're in for a swinging retro experience. What catches you off guard is the jovial hospitality. Don't be surprised if the owners drop around with freshly baked cookies. That friendly spirit seems contagious. Each room is fronted by a small patio where guests gather. Sociable conversations lead to impromptu cocktail parties and room tours. Eclectic and distinctive rooms strike a balance of eye-pleasing nostalgia and modern comfort. 503 S. Montezuma Street, 928-717-0157, www.themotorlodge.com.

You don't earn the title "Everybody's Hometown" without good front porches, and the Hotel Vendome has dandies—shady patios with rocking chairs. Located downtown, but far enough from Whiskey Row to assure a restful night, guests enjoy old-fashioned hospitality in an intimate setting that's a cross be-tween bed and breakfast and boutique hotel. Built in 1917, this two-story landmark even has a resident ghost and ghost cat. 230 S. Cortez Street, (888) 468-3583, www.vendomehotel.com.

WHISKEY ROW

Even though the town of Prescott has sprawled in recent years, ambling off willy-nilly across rolling hills, its downtown core retains a distinctive charm. The stately courthouse and tree-draped lawn form an old-fashioned town square. Surrounding the plaza are galleries, shops, restaurants, and Whiskey Row, a stretch of Montezuma Street once packed shoulder to shoulder with saloons. This was where legendary figures like Wyatt and Virgil Earp and Doc Holliday drank. Plenty of historic watering holes still remain, including The Palace, Arizona's oldest frontier saloon. In 1900, when fire swept through Whiskey Row, custom-ers of The Palace carried the ornately carved 1880s Brunswick bar across the street to safety. Then they continued to toss back the hooch. Now that's a great drinking story.

Left: A sweep of shoreline along Watson Loop Trail. **Right:** A Watson Lake detour to Secret Cove delivers as advertised.

NO 12 Watson Lake Loop, Prescott

This is hands down my favorite hike in Prescott. The final piece was added in 2012, completing the loop. A series of connected trails encircles the sparkling lake, weaving through the Granite Dells, a stony wonderland of massive boulders, weathered and piled into exotic formations, like the Flintstones holding a yard sale.

There are lots of places to access the loop, but I start in Watson Lake Park. From the parking lot, I turn right on the trail. Some road noise follows you on this segment and I like to get it out of the way, but it's still a beautiful stretch of lake vistas. Signs and maps at each junction keep you pointed in the right direction. Big cottonwood trees cradle the southern toe of the water and wrap around Granite Creek. This lush spot is Watson Woods Riparian Preserve. The 126-acre preserve harbors the largest patch of riparian forest left in Prescott. Some of the big cottonwoods are over a century old.

I emerge from the preserve onto Peavine, a wide thoroughfare along the eastern bank popular with bikers, joggers, and stroller-pushing moms. The Peavine is part of the Rails-to-Trails Conservancy, a national program converting old railway beds into user-friendly paths. The Peavine continues for a few miles but I peel off onto Lakeshore Trail

at the first opportunity. This dirt singletrack skirts the edge of the lake as it twists among the Dells. I take a couple of short detours from the Lakeshore, because what hiker worth his boots can resist trails called Treehouse Loop and Secret Cove?

There's an enticing wildness to this side of the lake, a maze of rock domes, accessorized with yucca and cactus, oak and pine. The toothy granite formations rising above the lake make this an unforgettable hike. Expect to spend plenty of time gawking and gaping.

Over the Hill Trail cuts right through the Dells, in and out of rocky gullies, until it dips into a marshy swath at the base of Watson Dam. Water gushes from the mid-section of the dam, creating a corridor of tangled wetlands shaded by cottonwoods and willows. The Northshore Trail is the newest addition, clambering up a steep rock face and delivering stunning panoramas. It traces the water's edge back to my starting point.

Where: From downtown Prescott, travel north on Arizona 89 for approximately 5 miles to Watson Lake Park. Turn right into the park and follow the road until it dead ends.

Cost: $2 fee per vehicle. Free on Wednesday.
Difficulty: Moderate.
Length: 4.8-mile loop.
Details: (928) 777-1121, www.prescotttrails.com.

Brown Bag Burger

PRESCOTT

If you leave Brown Bag Burger hungry, have yourself checked for a tapeworm. The smallest burger on the menu weighs in at seven ounces. Ponder that for a moment. Just under a half-pound slab of meat qualifies as dainty. From there they ratchet up to 10, 14, and a monstrous 20-ouncer. Not to mention that all shakes and malts of hand-scooped ice cream are 28 ounces. The perfect size to share in a double-straw, heads-together, romantic '50s flashback.

Tucked away in a strip mall, this little spot would be easy to miss. But all you have to do is follow the lunch crowds that pack the place. All burgers are made from premium ground chuck, pattied fresh daily. They're dragged through the garden and surrounded by fries. They also serve a selection of chicken, shrimp, fish, and a Polish dog. 150 E. Sheldon Street, (928) 445-3353.

№ 13 Sycamore Rim, Williams

I always forget how much I like this trail. Then I spend an idyllic summer day hiking it and can't believe I stayed away so long. The mostly level pathway traces a lumpy circle through sprawling meadows and pine forests that part long enough to provide panoramas of high-walled Sycamore Canyon.

There are five major trailheads for Sycamore Rim, but I start from the most accessible. Take the trail clockwise heading toward Dow Spring. Cut across a deep grass meadow ringed by ponderosa pines. You soon brush past the ruins of a century-old sawmill and Dow Spring, which was once a welcome water stop on the old Overland Road. A few cabin ruins remain, and though it's hard to imagine in this lonely spot, Dow Spring once had its own post office.

Past the cabins, the trail drops into a shallow canyon cradling a series of small pools that in

Fast Fact: The town of Williams was named after "Old Bill" Williams, a legendary mountain man, guide, and fur trapper who spoke several Indian languages. He lived among friendly tribes and survived numerous scrapes with warring factions until he was finally killed in 1849 by a band of Utes.

SWEET SUMMER RAIN I live in a dry place where rain is always a welcome guest, a cause for celebration. Timely rain is like an autograph from God. Especially those fierce monsoon storms of summer that roll in as we're choking on dust and heat.

I have a rule that if I'm home on a summer day and it starts to rain after 4 p.m., all work stops. I sit on my back porch with a beverage to cheer on the proceedings. I savor the perfume released and the pounding on the roof, the relentless rat-a-tat of wet shrapnel. Raindrops impale themselves on cactus spines and sometimes pools begin to gather in the arroyo behind my house. I've even been known to break into an impromptu rain dance to coax additional moisture from the skies. No telling how many times my wife has come home from work to find me soaking wet and smelling of beer. She's living the dream, people.

Sycamore Point offers dazzling views near Sycamore Rim Trail. **Below**: Pomeroy Tanks are a happy, wet surprise on Sycamore Rim.

summer are filled with water lilies. I spend a lot of time hiking Arizona trails and trust me when I say that water lilies are not exactly a common sight. I tend to sit here at water's edge awhile, just gazing at the floating lilies and their gaudy blossoms. I like to keep track of small miracles.

You get lots of different looks over the next couple of miles—copses of oaks, then airy ponderosa forests, and swatches of rippling prairies. Near the halfway point of Vista Point, you can scan the dense woods cloaking Sycamore Canyon below. Soon afterward, you arrive at Sycamore Falls. Very

occasionally you'll find water tumbling but more often you'll see rock climbers making their ascent on the perpendicular walls, and hopefully no tumbling is involved.

The trail veers away from the canyon and rambles through Pomeroy Tanks, some lovely perennial pools in another shallow canyon. From here you start to climb KA Hill, the only serious workout of the journey. But crossing the 7,287-foot summit, you'll have good views all the way to the San Francisco Peaks. From here, the trail switchbacks down the slope, a mile back to the trailhead.

Where: From Flagstaff, go west on Interstate 40 nearly 30 miles. Take Exit 167 (Garland Prairie Road) and turn south on Forest Road 141. Roughly 9 miles from I-40, turn right on FR 56. Follow FR 56 for 1.5 miles to the signed trailhead.

Cost: Free. **Difficulty:** Moderate. **Length:** 11 miles. **Details:** (928) 635-5600, www.fs.usda.gov/kaibab.

Fast Fact: At twenty miles long and seven miles wide, Sycamore is the second-largest canyon in the state. If you're curious as to the biggest, it's the one we call Grand.

Steep walls near Sycamore Falls are popular with climbers.

Twisters 50's Soda Fountain   WILLIAMS

The décor leans heavily on a color combo of red and white with a strong Coca-Cola theme. Lots of vintage Coke signs plaster the walls, and Coke chairs are at the tables. Burgers are quarter-pound patties, but you can double up on the meat by ordering the Big Bopper.

My combo arrives in a red plastic basket, a gang of shoestring fries and burger wrapped in paper. I'm a sucker for a paper-wrapped burger. Such a simple thing, I know, but it just takes me back. It's like unwrapping a gift of juicy beef. And since this is a genuine soda fountain, if you want a shake, malt, cherry Coke, root beer float, Brooklyn egg cream, or some other fizzy/creamy concoction, they can whip it up. I think everything is good. I brought my dad here and he raved about the steak. But come on . . . a burger and a cherry Coke? Tell me you're not thinking about it now. 417 E. Route 66, (928) 635-0266, www.route66place.com.

THE SEDUCTION OF NEON

Route 66 didn't invent the neon sign but it certainly perfected it. And Williams has a great concentration of neon strung through their compact downtown. After my hike and my burger, I like to roam the streets of Williams. Once the sun goes down, the soft knife of neon carves the twilight into rainbow hues. The whole burg is awash in a liquid velvet glow. Neon is the nightlight of angels and drunkards.

All the shops, restaurants, and bars stay open late, with music spilling out of every doorway. I sit on a patio listening to a few tunes and sipping a beer from Grand Canyon Brewing Co. here in town. The sidewalks are bustling, traffic slow-rumbles up and down Route 66, and it's one of my favorite carefree summer evenings. My hike becomes much more than just a walk in the woods.

ROOMS WITH A VIEW

The great thing about camping is that it provides access to seclusion and serenity. The bad thing is . . . you're camping. There's the whole sleeping on the ground business and battling the elements. Yet thanks to the Rooms with a View cabin rental program, visitors to Arizona's national forests can hit the backcountry and still enjoy a bed and other comforts of home.

Several years ago the forest service began sprucing up historic cabins and renting them out. There are several across the state including Spring Valley Cabin located 25 miles east of Williams. You'll understand how the Rooms with a View program got its name soon as you arrive at the 90-year-old cabin that crouches at the wind-brushed edge of an alpine meadow. You'll feel blessed to have a yard extending to the horizon. Just don't get so over-protective you start yelling at grazing mule deer to get off your lawn. (928) 635-8200, www.fs.usda.gov/kaibab.

TOP 5 REASONS NOT TO HIKE

5. Lost hiking boots in a game of strip poker.

4. Will hurt your chances of getting into the Guinness Book of World Records as Most Sedentary Person.

3. Electronic ankle monitor alerts authorities whenever you leave the yard.

2. All those episodes of Law & Order on the DVR aren't going to watch themselves.

1. Uneven terrain could cause you to spill your margarita.

GRAND CANYON

NOTHING PREPARES YOU for the wallop of the Grand Canyon. That first glimpse is so beyond scope and precedent, it devastates you. Yet the whole shebang stays hidden from view, sheltered by a thin screen of forest, until you're practically on top of it. You know you're getting close as you approach. The trees waver and then break apart against a wall of sky as the world abruptly ends.

Standing at the high crest of an overlook, a collapsed mosaic of terraces and buttes spreads below in an endless pattern, finally dissolving into a lavender haze. There should be a state law that every Arizona resident must visit the Grand Canyon at least once. It will be the first piece of legislation I enact when I'm elected governor.

№ 14 Bright Angel–Tonto–South Kaibab Loop, South Rim

Don't even think about this entire route as a day hike unless you're physically fit, experienced, and acclimated to the Grand Canyon. This is an extremely difficult and potentially dangerous outing. Try short hikes down the Bright Angel to develop your canyon legs first. Then explore the

Ever-changing light and shadows wash over the Grand Canyon.

South Kaibab. You should plan to tackle the Tonto Loop only after you've made multiple forays below the rim and know the terrain and your capabilities. But I warn you; dipping your toe into the Big Ditch can be extremely addictive.

The easiest way to tackle this long loop is to descend on the Kaibab, cut across the Tonto, and return via Bright Angel.

Screamingly steep, shadeless, and sunbeaten may not sound like endorsements but it's what makes the South Kaibab astounding. Most canyon trails follow fault lines limiting your range of vision. But South Kaibab only briefly hugs the upper cliffs before breaking free. At 0.9 miles it elbows into the canyon at aptly named Ooh Aah Point. From here the Kaibab skitters down a narrow ridge and offers virtually unobstructed views up and down the abyss.

At 1.5 miles you reach a comfy plateau called Cedar Ridge, complete with restrooms and great sitting rocks. Most day-trippers turn around here. Dropping, the trail curves past O'Neill Butte and approaches Skeleton Point, a jut of stone atop the Redwall Limestone.

At Skeleton Point, three miles from the trailhead, you get your first glimpse of the Colorado River. You'll find an excellent perch on the western

Expect scant shade but sprawling vistas on South Kaibab.

side of the promontory. Relax and soak it all in. From here the trail drops through a natural break in the Redwall in a series of steep switchbacks, depositing you on the scrubby Tonto Platform. Known as the Tipoff, there's another toilet here and an emergency telephone, just past the junction of the Tonto Trail.

Turn west on the Tonto, following the rangy benchland through the belly of the canyon. The Tonto Platform hangs on the rim of the Inner Gorge and is a place of immense peace and solitude. I'm never happier on a trail than when I'm hiking the Tonto. I'm a speck amid the vastness, but a mighty speck, drunk on panoramas of towers and temples and the occasional glimpse of the river.

For ninety-five miles this transcanyon route parallels the course of the Colorado. Less traveled sections are often faint and overgrown, but the 4.6-mile link between South Kaibab and Bright Angel is clearly defined. The trail undulates in and out of washes and skirts the edges of deep box canyons.

A smattering of trees marks two trickling stream crossings at Burro Springs and Pipe Creek. Otherwise, expect a sunbaked landscape of blackbrush, bunch grass, and tumbled boulders. So much of the Grand Canyon is about angles. We're accustomed by rim-top views to see certain geometric patterns.

Fast Fact: The Bright Angel Trail was once a privately operated toll road.

The Tonto flips everything sideways.

Tonto connects with Bright Angel Trail amid a grove of cottonwood trees below the spring-fed oasis of Indian Garden. Drinking water, privies, picnic tables, and shade make this a welcome rest stop. But after the solitude of the Tonto you'll encounter a jarring amount of humanity. Campers, backpackers, and mule riders will be enjoying the same amenities.

Leaving Indian Garden, you'll have about a half-mile of Bright Angel tilted gently uphill and just as you start thinking this won't be so bad, you bang into the unforgiving Redwall. A string of switchbacks known as Jacob's Ladder follow a broken fault line, climbing these sheer cliffs.

Three Mile Resthouse perches atop the Redwall, where there is another chance to use the can, and water is available in summer months. The same goes for Mile-and-a-Half Resthouse further up the trail. The last few miles are exhausting, coming at the end of a long day. Take your time and grind it out. Bright Angel emerges next to Kolb Studio in Grand Canyon Village.

Where: Trailhead is south of Yaki Point. The road is closed to private vehicles. Free shuttle provides access.

Cost: $25 entrance fee per vehicle.
Difficulty: Strenuous.
Length: 13.6 miles round-trip.
Details: (928) 638-7888, www.nps.gov/grca.

Bright Angel Soda Fountain

GRAND CANYON VILLAGE

This is my traditional stop after a long canyon hike, where I grab a couple of hot dogs. It's a cute place at the back of historic Bright Angel Lodge. The dogs are foil-wrapped inside a steam cabinet. They're pretty standard issue, but trust me, after a grueling climb out of the Big Ditch, these dogs will taste like you're sitting behind the dugout during the seventh game of the World Series with your team up by four.

You know you're hiking the Grand Canyon when traversing the South Kaibab.

Along the Way...

CANYON VISTAS MULE RIDE

Concessioner Xanterra now offers the four-mile Canyon Vistas Mule Ride, the only single-day ride at the South Rim. Canyon Vistas ambles first through the woods and then bam! You're right at the edge, though not in a scary stirrup-hanging-over-the-abyss kind of way. The well-constructed trail sits comfortably back from the rim yet stays close enough to spark a holy-cow-I'm-peering-right-into-the-canyon feeling. From there it follows the canyon rim east, with spectacular views.

Over 600,000 people have taken the "long-eared taxis" since they were first offered at the Grand Canyon in 1887. The mules have become a defining tradition at the canyon. Now visitors can experience a historic mule ride, be finished by lunchtime, and not walk around bow-legged the rest of the day. (888) 297-2757, www.grandcanyonlodges.com.

PERSPECTIVE

I was not a huge fan of *The Flintstones*, preferring the great writing and detail rich animation of Bugs Bunny and his amigos. Still, a good gag is a good gag. In one *Flintstones* episode, while Fred and Wilma and Barney and Betty Rubble are on a road trip, they make a quick detour to see the Grand Canyon. As they stand there, Wilma sniffs that it doesn't look like much to her. We pan down to see a thin trickle of water running through an inch-high gulley at their feet. "Not now," replies Fred. "But they expect it to be a big thing someday."

GRAND SOLITUDE

Here's my strategy for the Tonto Loop: I drive to Yaki Point where the Kaibab is located in the pre-dawn. The road is closed to private vehicles, but a free shuttle provides access. However, I arrive before the first shuttle. There's a small picnic area near the turnoff. I park there and make the short walk through the woods by flashlight. The path is easy to follow.

I start down the Kaibab with pale limestone switchbacks outlined by the inky blackness. It is beyond the wee hours, and I march toward the fine revolution of dawn. Cliff walls shake off the darkness as the rocks begin to shimmer, hard mauve then soft pink. I'm deep in the canyon by the time the sun gouges a rosy hole in the sky.

What's so great about this plan is the seclusion it affords me. I'm the first person on the South Kaibab and then across the seldom-traveled Tonto, and often I don't see another human until I reach Indian Gardens. So for several hours I have one of the Seven Natural Wonders of the World entirely to myself. That's worth setting the alarm clock.

MARY ELIZABETH JANE COLTER

Architect Mary Elizabeth Jane Colter was America's most influential female designer and revolutionized Southwestern construction. Her buildings were indigenous and organic, growing out of their surroundings. The bulk of Colter's surviving work can be found in Arizona, including the elegant La Posada Hotel in Winslow and many of the most notable Grand Canyon structures like Bright Angel Lodge, Hopi House, Lookout Studio, Hermit's Rest, Phantom Ranch, and Desert View Watchtower.

Near the eastern entrance of the national park perches a 70-foot-high lighthouse-shaped cylinder of rock known as the Watchtower. Designed in 1932, Colter recreated Ancestral Pueblo towers found throughout the Southwest. Remarkable stonework is wrapped around a concealed steel frame. The tower rises as an open shaft with circular balconies overlooking the central space. Slender curving stairways climb to the top, where visitors enjoy rapturous views from an enclosed observation deck.

Desert View Watchtower.

Vishnu Temple rises above Horseshoe Mesa. **Below:** Grandview Trail required impressive engineering.

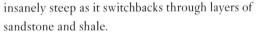

№15 Grandview Trail, South Rim

So I've done this a few times over the years: I get up early and drive to the Grand Canyon. I hike down the Grandview Trail to a little spot I know. I have lunch overlooking the inner canyon, hike back out, and I'm home in time for dinner. Know why I do it? Because I can! I live in this astonishing state where such a day is possible.

At Grandview Point, prospector Pete Berry built a trail in the 1890s that led to his mine on Horseshoe Mesa. Upper sections are still braced by logs and steel rods and you'll be hugging limestone in places where the trail squeezes skinny. Footing is occasionally tricky over segments of cobbled rock, but the views, as advertised, are quite tasty. The steep grade eases slightly after the first mile to the point where it's only

insanely steep as it switchbacks through layers of sandstone and shale.

It's three taxing miles to the remains of the Last Chance Mine on Horseshoe Mesa, where camping is allowed with a backcountry permit. Rocky ruins of the old cookhouse and a few artifacts scattered about are all that remain of the former mining camp. Please leave everything undisturbed for others to enjoy. There's a signed trail to an eco-friendly and very exposed toilet. You won't have much privacy but the panoramas more than compensate. You'll notice other trails dropping over the edge through the Redwall Limestone to connect with the Tonto Trail or Cottonwood Creek hundreds of feet below. Day hikers stay atop the mesa.

If you've still got some gas in your tank after your arduous descent, follow a rocky path along the western

The Colorado River flows past Phantom Ranch and beneath the Silver Bridge.

arm of the butte for another mile until it dead-ends dramatically 2,000 feet above the Colorado River. There's a piñon-shaded ledge where you can savor the aching stillness of distant backcountry. If you find me there eating lunch, scram. Find your own spot.

After the hike, I'm heading home. If you're still hungry, grab a bite at Desert View Snack Bar. And if you want a great sunset viewing spot, nearby Lipan Point is one of my favorite overlooks. I witnessed a fantastic sunset there once. Maybe you'll get lucky too.

Where: Trailhead is off Desert View Drive, 12 miles east of Grand Canyon Village.

Cost: $25 entrance fee per vehicle.

Difficulty: Strenuous.

Length: 6 miles round-trip to Horseshoe Mesa.

Details: (928) 638-7888, www.nps.gov/grca.

N0 16 North Kaibab Trail, North Rim

If you've only visited the South Rim, don't be alarmed by the lack of crowds here. A blanketing serenity is normal on this side of the trench, which receives a fraction of the visitors as the South Rim. Only 10 miles apart as the raven flies, it's a 215-mile drive from rim to rim. Rising 1,000 feet higher than its southern counterpart, the North Rim sits atop the Kaibab Plateau and is crowned with mixed conifer forest and lush grassy meadows. Frequent and heavy snowstorms close this section of the park during winter months.

The North Kaibab Trail plunges steeply from the start, dropping from big timber and twisting through Roaring Springs Canyon. At 1.7 miles you'll reach Supai Tunnel, where you'll find restrooms and water. This makes a good turnaround point

Hot Tip Anyone who spends time staring into the Earth's most gaping wound and doesn't have a few geology questions isn't paying attention. The exhibits at Yavapai Geology Museum provide the answers, and the expansive windows provide spectacular views. Located near Yavapai Point in the Village.

Hikers descend on the mighty North Kaibab Trail.

North Kaibab is cruelly steep and relentlessly spectacular.

if your time is limited or your knees are grouchy. You'll glide down the switchbacks, but they somehow quadruple in number on the way back up.

I love zigzagging down the Redwall Limestone, a lightning bolt of trail clinging to sheer cliffs. The trees have dispersed and this section offers expansive views and thrilling exposure. Much of this corridor has been blasted from solid rock. This feels like a classic Grand Canyon experience, scrambling along a steep trail of remarkable engineering amid a soul-freeing backdrop.

You'll hear Roaring Springs before you see it, a frothy geyser bursting from the cliffs and cascading downhill to form Bright Angel Creek. The water source for all Grand Canyon National Park, Roaring Springs is absolutely the end of the line as a day hike. A 0.25-mile spur trail descends to picnic tables and restrooms tucked beneath a clutch of cottonwoods that thrive in this riparian setting formed by the springs. Make this a leisurely pit stop because you'll need to muster your resources for the 5-mile climb back to the trailhead.

Do NOT attempt to hike to the river and back

in a day. Over 250 people are rescued from the canyon each year. Don't become a casualty. Only those on a multi-night rim-to-rim hike or backpacking adventure should continue past Roaring Springs.

Be sure to make the short detour to Ribbon Falls, a magical oasis that looks like it was plucked from a tropical island. The silvery spray of water tumbles down rock walls in a picturesque grotto. It's another 2.5 miles to Cottonwood Camp and 9.4 miles to Phantom Ranch.

Where: From Grand Canyon Lodge, drive 2 miles north to the trailhead.

Cost: $25 entrance fee per vehicle.

Difficulty: Strenuous.

Length: 10 miles round-trip to Roaring Springs.

Details: (928) 638-7888, www.nps.gov/grca/.

"In wilderness I sense the miracle of life, and behind it our scientific accomplishments fade to trivia."

—CHARLES LINDBERGH

Hot Tip ❄ The 23-mile Cape Royal Road is a spectacular scenic drive with multiple canyon overlooks along the way, including a breathtaking view of the natural bridge known as Angels Window shown at top right of this photo.

Grand Canyon Lodge

The first time most people see the canyon at the North Rim it's indoors. (The people are indoors; the park service still keeps the canyon outside just like at the South Rim.) The highway ends at historic Grand Canyon Lodge, built right on the edge of the abyss. Walk through the front door to discover giant picture windows across the lobby filled with stunning views of the canyon.

Make reservations pronto if you plan to dine. A restaurant with a wall of windows gazing into a chasm fills up quickly. The menu has evolved in recent years and emphasizes contemporary and regional dishes like Arizona elk chili and fresh Utah trout. If you go the burger route, they've got an all-natural beef beauty. You can also try a bison burger, a leaner healthier alternative to beef. Sack lunches are available for hikers. (877) 386-4383, www.grandcanyonlodgenorth.com.

PHANTOM RANCH

Tucked away on the canyon floor, Phantom Ranch is one of the all-time great outposts—a scrap of civilization on the fringe of nowhere. Hard to reach and hard to leave, the collection of stone-walled buildings is scattered among cottonwood trees on the north side of the Colorado River. Built in 1922, Phantom can only be reached by mule, raft, or foot. Rustic cabin and dormitory accommodations are available, and there's a nearby campground. The canteen sells snacks, drinks, and supplies, and also acts as a dining hall for breakfast and dinner.

Be aware though, both meals and beds are booked a year in advance. But if your schedule is limber you can often catch a cancellation. Since I live in the vicinity and am only vaguely employed, I just call and ask what dates are open. I book one and plan my trip around that. (888) 297-2757, www.grandcanyonlodges.com.

GRAND CANYON FIELD INSTITUTE

Visitors to the Grand Canyon are often overwhelmed trying to grasp the immensity of the place. Even a few minutes at a crowded viewpoint pops the eyes wide and sends the mind reeling. The Grand Canyon Field Institute personalizes this geological masterpiece through guided and educational outings. The nonprofit organization is part of the Grand Canyon Association, an official partner of the National Park Service. Each year GCFI conducts over 200 classes. They do what the rangers would like to do, if they had the time and the funding.

Classes are exploratory adventures that range from rim-to-rim backpacking hikes, float trips down the Colorado River, mule-assisted camping, geology and archaeology studies, photography workshops, and rimside yoga sessions. They can be as short as a couple of hours or last for several days, but each is designed to enhance the visitor experience at the Grand Canyon. www.grandcanyon.org/fieldinstitute.

Widforss Trail rambles through North Rim forests. **Below:** Tasty canyon views peek through all along the Widforss.

NO 17 Widforss Trail, North Rim

I feel like an idiot for not knowing this already, but here's my big take-away from this trail: Lupines smell delicious! I never thought of lupines as having a distinct fragrance, but when the Widforss cut through great swaths of the blue wildflowers, the aroma staggered me—a scent reminiscent of amped-up lilacs. I actually lay down in the middle of the path, inhaling for several minutes. Fortunately, no one else happened along just then.

Not every trail at the canyon is a grueling death march. The Widforss, for example, never dips

below the rim. Named for Gunnar Widforss, an artist who painted western national parks in the 1920s and 1930s, the trail rambles through shaggy woods, offering big canyon panoramas on the way. Near the trailhead, grab a brochure from the metal box. The guide matches up with numbered markers scattered along the first 2.5 miles of the hike identifying points of interest.

Fast Fact: All visitor facilities at the North Rim are closed from mid-October to mid-May.

Much of this segment traces the edge of the gorge, so you'll enjoy impressive viewpoints. The final marker is one such overlook. You can head back after that for a nice 5-miler. If you continue, the trail turns into the forest, cutting through a picturesque little valley where I had my lupine epiphany. Even though it was early in the monsoon season, blooms were splashed across the forest floor. I spotted fleabane, paintbrush, fireweed, and several others I couldn't readily identify.

On the approach to Widforss Point, a picnic

Widforss Trail is easy on your knees but fiercely squeezes your heart.

table sits in the shade of a big ponderosa pine. It has to be the most superfluous picnic table in the park. Who's going to drive to the North Rim, hike five miles into the woods, then stop a few feet from the rim—where there are no canyon vistas—to have a picnic?

Fast Fact: The Grand Canyon is 277 miles long, up to 18 miles wide, and over a mile deep.

My suggestion is to continue walking the additional fifty yards to Widforss Point. There you can find a nice sitting rock with terrific views and have yourself a proper canyon-side repast. Remember: friends don't let friends picnic irresponsibly.

Where: From Grand Canyon Lodge, drive 2.6 miles north to the signed turnoff. Turn left on the gravel road and proceed to the parking area.

Cost: $25 entrance fee per vehicle.

Difficulty: Moderate.

Length: 10 miles round-trip.

Details: (928) 638-7888, www.nps.gov/grca/.

LOOKIN' OUT MY BACK DOOR

The first house we bought in Arizona was because of the back porch. We walked in the front door and I kept going straight out the back. My wife got the grand tour from the realtor and finally came looking for me. I was ready to make an offer without knowing whether the house had a kitchen or bathroom. It had a porch with a spectacular view of Mingus Mountain. I had a mountain right out my back door. I was living in a Credence Clearwater Revival song.

Patio, porch, balcony, veranda—however it's qualified, that's where I want to sit. It's a room, yet it's outside. What's not to love? A porch shades you from the sun but lets you experience the warmth. It shelters you from the rain but lets you feel the spray of the water. Porches are Zen structures, self-contained worlds beyond the reach of dilemma and despair. Having a porch attached to one's home is what truly separates us from the animals.

Lees Ferry Lodge at Vermilion Cliffs

MARBLE CANYON

This rustic inn sits on one of the loneliest and most scenic highways in Arizona, just south of the Utah state line. Tucked against a ferocious escarpment of towering rock walls, Lees Ferry Lodge offers motel rooms, a restaurant, and a bar with an amazing beer selection. I can't vouch for the rooms because I haven't spent the night but I can never drive by without grabbing a bite and a brew and to relax for a while on one of my favorite front porches in the world.

The Vermilion Cliffs rise 3,000 feet above the plateau, a geological upheaval that appears as an endless line of lofty buttes and mesas. Carved by eons of erosion to expose a bouquet of colorful strata, the cliffs provide your meal with an unforgettable backdrop. You can't go wrong with ribs, steaks, the delicious smoked trout platter, or big ol' burger. But it's the porch I love most. Sitting there on a June evening as the twilight unpeels the afternoon heat and the sky spins through a color wheel—red, then orange, then melting into a molten puddle of gold—is the ideal way to kiss summer full on the lips. Milepost 541.5 Arizona 89A, (928) 355-2231, www.vermilioncliffs.com.

Fast Fact: The only place where the United States Post Office still delivers mail by mule is the village of Supai, located at the bottom of the Grand Canyon.

JACOB LAKE

The North Rim Parkway (Arizona 67) begins in the hamlet of Jacob Lake. While little more than a busy corner, this still qualifies as the main commercial district between the North Rim and Kanab, Utah. Historic Jacob Lake Inn offers motel rooms and cabins. They also sell gasoline and operate a general store, soda fountain, lunch counter, and bakery. Be sure to stop and grab a sack of fresh-baked cookies. They've got classic flavors and also some weird but yummy combos. Your sweet tooth will thank you. (928) 643-7232, www.jacoblake.com.

UTAH BORDER

THE IMMENSE DIVERSITY of the state is on display as you travel north across tribal lands. The Navajo and Hopi reservations blanket Arizona's northeast quadrant, where you'll find an other-worldly landscape of lonely plateaus, colorful sandstone cliffs, and deep-cut canyons. Along the far northern edge are two remarkable destinations—the towering buttes of Monument Valley and the azure waters of cliff-lined Lake Powell, both straddling the border with Utah, the second most beautiful state in the union behind only... well, you know.

Beyond the scenery, the journey provides a chance to experience vibrant indigenous cultures. Take some time to learn about the history and traditions of the people who live here and their deep connections to the land.

Nº 18 Hanging Garden Trail, Page

Page is the gateway to Lake Powell, which has nearly 2,000 miles of shoreline, more than the entire west coast of the continental United States. Yet one of the loveliest hikes in town leads to a pool of water so small it wouldn't fill a cactus wren's bathtub.

The magnificent desolation of Monument Valley.

A wide path lined by river rocks cuts across open sand to the base of Manson Mesa. From here the trail bends left and skirts the edge of the slope. Big views roll back over the broken lands toward the dam and a sliver of lake.

Lake Powell exists because of Glen Canyon Dam. Construction of the 710-foot-tall stone arch dam was completed in 1963 and began corralling the waters of the volatile Colorado River. It took seventeen years for Lake Powell to completely fill. While the purpose of the dam was to provide

Hot Tip Learn about Native American culture at the Explore Navajo Museum in Tuba City. Exhibits touch on creation stories, ceremonial life, and family systems. The museum is adjacent to Tuba City Trading Post and Navajo Code Talkers Museum. www.discovernavajo.com.

water storage and to generate power, it has also created uncanny drama in the middle of nowhere. This epic reservoir spreads across a land carved and scraped, twisted and torn, as if the cosmos continues to tinker with it. Rock walls and columns rise abruptly from sapphire waters. Submerged towers and castles appear at every bend of the lake. Atlantis does exist; its skyline lies hidden beneath the Southwestern desert.

A bit of sun followed by a splash of shade defines Hanging Garden Trail. **Below:** The Hanging Garden makes a luxuriant little desert oasis.

I follow the cairns on a short, gentle climb with the sun ricocheting off bare stone. The trail is hot and exposed, which makes the ending such a sweet payoff. Up and under the high shoulder of the mesa, a lush oasis awaits, tucked in a verdant alcove.

As I approach the recess, I'm smacked by a wave of cool air, like a cream pie in the kisser. The temperature drops sharply. More than just simple shade, this is an enveloping shade. I feel like I'm wearing a suit made out of shade with ice cubes stuffed in the pockets.

A dense mat of ferns forms a luxuriant cover across the entire back wall. Small orchids bloom amid the greenery created by a seep spring. This is the namesake hanging garden. A few stones surround a saucer-sized puddle, forming a mini-saloon for lizards. Several lurk nearby waiting for Happy Hour. I pull up a cool rock and join them.

Where: Drive through Page on U.S. 89. Just north of the city, 0.5 miles before the dam, there's a turn-off on the right with a brown hiker sign. Turn and follow the gravel road 0.2 miles to the signed kiosk.

Cost: Free.   **Difficulty:** Easy.

Length: 1 mile round-trip.

Details: (928) 608-6200, www.nps.gov/glca.

Ja'di'To'oh

ANTELOPE POINT MARINA

There's a great burger waiting nearby but you have to pay a cover charge to get in. It's actually the entrance fee to the Glen Canyon National Recreation Area. But if you made the drive to Page, you no doubt planned on visiting Lake Powell anyway, so start at Antelope Point Marina. Built in partnership with the Navajo Nation and National Park Service, Antelope Point is Lake Powell's newest marina. There's a public launch ramp, plus Marina Village, which is the largest floating platform in the world. That's where you'll find a lounge, retail store, and the lovely restaurant, Ja'di'To'oh—Navajo for "Antelope Springs."

The open breezeway and floor to ceiling glass walls make the whole place seem like a sprawling patio. Even when sitting indoors, it feels like you're outside. Natural light streams in from every angle, and your meal comes with a side of lake panoramas. The brawny burger is topped with cheddar cheese, bacon, and Hatch green chiles, so there's a nice spicy bite riding in at the tail end. (928) 645-5900, www.antelopepointlakepowell.com.

Fast Fact: Lake Powell is the second largest manmade lake in the United States. The largest is Lake Mead, also in Arizona.

"Looking hard for a drive-in, searching for a corner café, where the hamburgers sizzle on an open grill night and day."

—CHUCK BERRY

Along the Way...

HORSESHOE BEND

Treat yourself to an optical thunderbolt just south of Page. A short hike leads to Horseshoe Bend Overlook perched atop a steep cliff with the emerald-green Colorado River shimmering one thousand feet below. You'll have no trouble figuring out how this spot earned its name because the river makes a sweeping horseshoe-shaped curve. It is an eye-popping, jaw-dropping sight. Bring your wide-angle lens to capture it all. Use extreme caution when approaching the edge and keep control of children and pets. If you find heights daunting, try lying down on the ground and peering over the edge. The trailhead is located off U.S. 89, two miles south of Page.

LAKE POWELL

Humans are primarily land mammals, designed for land-based activities such as walking, running, and *Dancing with the Stars*. Swimming does not come naturally to any creature with feet instead of flippers. Staying away from deep water is prudent.

That's my boating philosophy in a nutshell. While I like being around water, I'm happier on shore. Still, I've done my share of kayaking and canoeing and have been out on Lake Powell in everything from a speedboat to a luxury houseboat with a hot tub on the upper deck, and it is pretty cool. Lake Powell meanders for 186 miles with 96 major canyons begging for a little exploration. You can rent all manner of watercraft from Antelope Point and Wahweap Marinas, or book one of their scenic cruises.

GOULDING'S LODGE

Although Goulding's Lodge sits just outside the boundary of Monument Valley Navajo Tribal Park, it is a crucial piece of the valley's history. It was Harry Goulding, operator of a trading post, who first brought the sprawling western landscape to the attention of John Ford. Goulding and his wife Leone, affectionately known as "Mike," first built rooms to provide accommodations to the film crews and actors. Goulding's Lodge, nestled at the base of a towering  butte, is a minitown today with grocery store, gas station, gift shop, restaurant, museum, and tours in open-air vehicles. Each night a small theater shows a movie filmed in Monument Valley, which is seriously fun. Southwestern-style rooms are clean and comfortable and come with private balconies. (435) 727-3231, www.gouldings.com.

A scenic dirt road snakes across the floor of Monument Valley.

№ 19   Wildcat Trail, Monument Valley

There are many ways to explore the radiant desolation of Monument Valley, but if you want a piece of it all to yourself, hike the Wildcat Trail. The Wildcat is the only trail within the Tribal Park that visitors can hike without a Navajo guide. It brushes so close to the iconic formations known as the Mittens, you can feel them holding you.

> **Hot Tip**   Park visitors can drive a rough, 17-mile dirt loop road through the heart of the park. Navajo-led tours are also available and well worth the cost. Remote sections of the park like Mystery Valley are accessible only by guided tour.

Starting from the campground below The View Hotel, the trail drops a few hundred feet to the valley floor. This feels like the edge of the world, where blocky towers vault from the sand and sagebrush and pierce a tall sky. It is hauntingly quiet here in the brittle afternoon light. I walk into the expanse, gazing at monoliths stranded like shipwrecks washed up on an ancient shore.

Curving through the gnarled scrub and wind-bent juniper trees, Wildcat loops around West Mitten. The Navajos have occupied these lands for centuries. Yet for generations of moviegoers like me it was director John Ford's grand-scale films that helped Monument Valley come to define the American West. His first movie set against this backdrop was the 1939 classic *Stagecoach*, elevating the genre and turning John Wayne into a breakout star. Orson Welles claimed to have watched *Stagecoach* more than forty times during the making of *Citizen Kane*. I probably see it that many times in a weekend if my wife goes out of town.

For a hike through such an unrelenting sweep of land, it is surprisingly intimate. The easy walking gives your eyes a chance to consume every detail. Small stacks of rock cairns and a few signs point the way. I move at a tarantula's pace, slow crawling across the sand, trying to make the miles last.

As I swung around from the backside of the formation, I had one of those small diamond-shaped moments that leave permanent fingerprints on your heart. Standing alone on a rise at the base of the Mitten, a horse grazed in the scrub. A chestnut, his coat almost liquid in the sun, he flicked his tail and cocked an eye my way. I stood for a long time and could hear no sound but his contented chomping. It was me and a horse, alone in Monument Valley. I was no longer watching westerns; I was living one.

I climbed from the valley floor, stopping to look back every few steps to reassure myself the horse hadn't dissolved into another desert mirage. As I reached the trailhead, the fading sun swabbed the stony plumes with a radiant glow. Deep rich reds washed down the formations, shimmering in still air. I felt like I was seeing the reflection of God's brake lights as He stopped to give me a smile.

Some days it just pays to get out and walk around. Hey, I think I'm hungry!

Where: Monument Valley Navajo Tribal Park is 175 miles northeast of Flagstaff. Take U.S. 89 north to U.S. 160. Turn right and proceed to Kayenta. Turn left on U.S. 163, go for 23 miles, and turn right into the park. Trail begins 0.4 miles north of visitor center from the campground.

Cost: There is a $5 per person entrance fee.

Difficulty: Moderate.   **Length:** 3.2 miles.

Details: (435) 727-5874, www.navajonationparks.org

The View Hotel

MONUMENT VALLEY

Perched on a mesa amidst towering monoliths, The View is the first hotel built inside Monument Valley Navajo Tribal Park. Designed to exist in harmony with the magnificent surroundings, the hotel stands only three stories tall, a low contour conforming to the mesa that overlooks the valley. The restaurant, just like most of the motel rooms, faces east toward prominent formations the Mittens and Merrick Butte. In a state with no shortage of dramatic settings, this one is hard to top.

Their burger is a solid half-pounder called—wait for it—the John Wayne. But while you're here, you should try some traditional dishes like the Navajo taco or the green chile stew, loaded with chunks of potatoes, carrots, and spicy pork.
(435) 727-5555,
www.monumentvalleyview.com.

Fast Fact: Unlike the rest of Arizona, daylight saving time is observed on the Navajo Nation.

MONUMENT VALLEY BALLOON COMPANY

Everyone wants to witness the sunrise in Monument Valley but only a fortunate few get to be part of it. Rise above the monoliths in a hot air balloon and meet the sun while it is still young and supple and bathing the landscape in golden hues. From May through December, Monument Valley Balloon Company picks up passengers from nearby motels during the predawn and drives to a launch site. (800) 843-5987, www.monumentvalleyballooncompany.com.

PHOENIX
AND THE
Central Deserts

EVERYONE IN ARIZONA lives within fifteen minutes of a trail. That's true even in the Valley of the Sun, which encompasses Phoenix and the surrounding cities like Scottsdale, Tempe, Glendale, and Mesa. Despite the sprawling urban setting, mountain parks and preserves are scattered through the cityscape, affording quick getaways to residents and visitors alike. With over two hundred miles of trails, this is some primo Sonoran Desert hiking.

North America has four major deserts. The Sonoran, defined by the stately saguaro cactus, dominates Arizona. It sweeps across the southern half of the state, dropping into Mexico and edging slightly across the California border. It's our personal playground, cherished by local desert rats. Heaven help me, I never intended to swoon for such a harsh landscape. Loving the desert is like being in a relationship with someone who constantly tries to kill you. Yet you always forgive them, and always come back for more.

№ 20 Cholla Trail, Camelback Mountain

The Phoenix skyline isn't defined by skyscrapers but by mountains. Scuffed, lumpy ranges rise from

A steep ascent up Cholla Trail doesn't deter Phoenix hikers.

every quadrant of the valley floor. One of the most prominent and certainly the most distinctive is Camelback Mountain, looming over tony 'hoods at the edge of Scottsdale.

Two hiking trails reach the summit of Camelback. The Cholla is slightly less steep and less crowded than the Echo Canyon route, although that's a relative comparison. As an urban trail, Cholla can still feel like a conga line of people snaking their way up the spine of the kneeling camel. And the last quarter-mile is cruelly steep, requiring scrambling, climbing, and prayer.

Even finding a parking spot can prove challenging. The trailhead is tucked away in a residential neighborhood off Cholla Lane where parking is verboten. You'll have to score one of the designated spots on Invergordon Road in front of the swanky Phoenician Resort, then hoof down Cholla, adding 10 minutes of walking to your hike.

Once you're on the well-marked trail, the first segment rounds the edge of the golf course and then curves back into the mountains, rising to a nice overlook of the resort. You wend your way up the long eastern ridge, climbing a few steep switchbacks before leveling off. The occasional saguaro crowds the path along with clumped boulders, foreshadowing the rocky conclusion lying ahead.

Just under a mile in, you reach a high saddle, a good place to catch your second wind. I don't recall needing a second wind as much in my youth. Now sometimes I need third through fifth winds. I don't know how many winds we have altogether, but as I age, I'm grateful for each and every one.

There's more climbing to another saddle. Gorgeous views keep getting better. Enjoy them here because once you make for the top you need to focus. The final pitch to the summit is a precipitous scramble across granite vertebrae. The trail is mostly theory at this point as you thread your way up and over boulders. Painted blue dots and reflectors help keep you on the easiest route. No technical skills are required, just short climbs up rock faces. Fortunately, the rough texture of the stone provides good foot traction and sturdy handholds.

All your efforts are rewarded when you reach the 2,704-foot summit and are treated to stupendous head-spinning views. You see what a furious clutter of mountains exist beyond the sprawling metropolitan area. Take a well-earned breather, pick out landmarks, and snap some photos.

Fast Fact: Arizona has 3,928 mountain peaks and summits, more than any of the other mountain states.

When you're ready to return, use caution. Climbing down can be trickier than climbing up. And remember uphill hikers have the right of way. With gravity now on your side, you'll be tempted to cannonball through the poor saps still slogging up the mountain. Show benevolence, lest the forces of the universe conspire to twist your ankle in karmic retribution.

Where: From Loop 101 in Phoenix, exit onto Chaparral Road and drive west for 3.2 miles until it dead ends at Invergordon Road. Parking is on the west side of Invergordon in designated spaces between Cholla Lane and Camelback Road. Walk west on Cholla Lane about a quarter-mile to the trailhead. There is no parking at the trailhead.

Cost: Free.   **Difficulty:** Strenuous.
Length: 3.6 miles round-trip.
Details: (602) 262-6862,
www.phoenix.gov/parks.

Pizzeria Bianco

PHOENIX

It's been many a long year since I've eaten my birthday dinner anywhere besides Pizzeria Bianco. And even though there are terrific pizza parlors close to home, my wife and I regularly make the two-hour drive to Bianco to experience a lunchtime of bliss. This is pizza nirvana and I'm far from the only one who thinks so. Pizzeria Bianco has been rated as the best pizza in the country by the *New York Times, Bon Appétit, Vogue,* Rachael Ray, and many others. Chris Bianco was the first pizza chef to win a James Beard Award and has been in the forefront of the artisanal pizza movement.

The downtown restaurant opened in 1996. A newer location in Town & Country Mall, slightly more convenient for us, has eliminated what was once an interminable wait for the exquisitely balanced pies. The creamy, homemade mozzarella and garden-fresh sauce sit atop a thin but puffy crust, which is charred, chewy, and rich as a dinner roll. A half dozen specialty combinations grace the menu. I'm devoted to the Sonny Boy, a smoky, crispy delight that's packed with thin slices of salami curled at the edges and Gaeta olives like dark, earthy jewels. 4743 N. 20th Street, (602) 368-3273, www.pizzeriabianco.com.

Fast Fact: The first barrel of tequila produced in the United States was in Nogales, Arizona, in 1936.

Freedom Trail hustles you away from the city into the desert.

No 21 Freedom Trail, Piestewa Peak

I can't imagine a more appropriate name for this trail that throws a lasso around Piestewa Peak. Right in the heart of town, it hustles you away from civilization and into lonesome desert in no time flat.

Rising to 2,608 feet, Piestewa Peak towers above the Phoenix Mountains Preserve. The trail to the summit is the Valley of the Sun's busiest trail, a teeming thoroughfare of sweaty humanity. The Freedom Trail circles the base of the mountain, and other than the short segment it shares with the Summit Trail, it is surprisingly deserted, a secret hiding in plain sight.

> **Fast Fact:** Formerly known as Squaw Peak, Piestewa Peak was renamed in honor of Arizona soldier Lori Piestewa, killed in action in Iraq in 2003. A member of the Hopi tribe, Piestewa was the first Native American woman killed in combat in a foreign war.

Once you enter Phoenix Mountains Preserve, you can access the Freedom Trail from several points. Parking areas near the summit trailhead will often be crowded. No need to jostle for a spot. Continue a little farther to one of the other lots.

Cross the wash that runs like an out-of-service moat at the base of the mountain and scramble up the other side where you'll find the Freedom Trail #302. Hang a right. The Freedom shares its route with other trails, so you'll see them joining and departing at various junctions. Just follow the 302 markers and remember you're circling Piestewa Peak so keep the mountain over your left shoulder.

The trail begins climbing, passing informational signage and a memorial bench as it points toward a prominent saddle. The saddle is the high point of the trail where more benches give you a chance to pause and enjoy long views.

Descending from the notch, the trail cuts across the slope through a cluster of jagged rock formations. This is my favorite section. I skip the benches and dawdle through here, enjoying the angular eye candy thrusting in all directions. Even in the middle of the city this trail snatches you from the mundane and gives you a taste of mystery. I never tire of that feeling. In Arizona, you never have to go far to get your heart squeezed.

It's a long traverse for the next mile overlooking residential neighborhoods. Then another climb to a saddle as it swings back around the mountain. At the crest you join the bustling Summit Trail, which is more of an open-air gym than hiking route. Among the crowd you'll likely see lots of toned, fit people in carefully selected outfits. They even sweat in a sultry manner. Scramble down the rocky ledges to the bottom of the hill and head back to your car.

Where: In Phoenix, exit Arizona 51 (Piestewa Freeway) at Lincoln Drive. Head east for 0.5 miles on Lincoln and turn left on Squaw Peak Drive. Proceed into the preserve.

Cost: Free.

Difficulty: Moderate.

Length: 3.7-mile loop.

Details: (602) 262-6862, www.phoenix.gov/parks.

Along the Way...

RESORTS

Walking past **The Phoenician** might encourage you to live it up a little. The Phoenix area is loaded with resorts, so whether you want old-school luxury or contemporary glitz, there's a pillow mint and heated toilet seat somewhere with your name on it.

The Phoenician

Besides the regal elegance and impeccable service that define The Phoenician ((480) 941-8200, www.thephoenician. com) here are a few others to consider.

Arizona Biltmore—This architectural gem was opened in 1929, inspired by a Frank Lloyd Wright design, and sprawls across thirty-nine acres of manicured grounds and colorful gardens. (602) 955-6600, www.arizonabiltmore.com.

Sanctuary on Camelback Mountain Resort and Spa—Terraced high on Camelback Mountain, this boutique resort offers panoramic views from spacious suites and casitas. (480) 948-2100, www.sanctuaryoncamelback.com.

Westin Kierland Resort & Spa—All beautifully appointed rooms have balconies or patios with views of the mountains or the resort's exquisite, kid-loved water park. (480) 624-1000, www.kierlandresort.com.

Hotel Valley Ho—This mid-century modern landmark dishes up a retro-chic and absolutely fabulous experience amid oversize, posh rooms and stylish grounds. (480) 248-2000, www.hotelvalleyho.com.

Hotel Valley Ho

HEARD MUSEUM

Anyone with an interest in the indigenous peoples of Arizona should plan a trip to the Heard Museum. Galleries showcasing historical and contemporary Native art have won the Heard international acclaim. What began as a private collection has grown to include a stunning array of jewelry, textiles, pottery, paintings, and more. Their beautiful gift shop is stocked with goods purchased directly from Native artists. (602) 252-8840, www.heard.org.

TALIESIN WEST

Spread across the foothills of the McDowell Mountains, Taliesin West was built by architect Frank Lloyd Wright as a winter camp. Work began in 1937. Today, the National Historic Landmark houses Wright's architecture school and offers public tours. The clustered buildings mirror the shapes and colors of the rugged desert that Wright found so intriguing. Using local stone and low profiles, and integrating indoor and outdoor spaces, the enclave coexists harmoniously with its surroundings. Many of the buildings are linked by dramatic terraces, gardens, and walkways. Tours of the 500-acre complex are offered year round and range from one to three hours. (480) 860-2700, www.franklloydwright.org.

TEMPE TOWN LAKE

Sailboats in the middle of the desert, in the heart of the metropolitan area, are enough to prompt a double take. Yet there they are, drifting across Tempe Town Lake, along with kayaks, hydrobikes, and stand-up paddleboards. Nearly two miles long with inflatable dams at each end, the lake fills the Salt River channel and acts as a central hub for city events. The paved pathways wrapping around the water are popular with walkers, joggers, and inline skaters. Illuminated bridges create a colorful nighttime display as an array of lights skitters off the surface. Tempe Town Lake is located just north of downtown Tempe and Arizona State University. (480) 350-8625, www.tempe.gov/lake.

Chicago Hamburger Company

PHOENIX

We all have guilty pleasures. Mine is sliders from White Castle. Those small square patties steam-cooked on a bed of onions have one of the most distinctive flavor profiles in all of burgerdom. Like a first love, you never forget them. There are no White Castle restaurants in Arizona, yet a craving can be satisfied with a visit to Chicago Hamburger Company. Walk in and discover a slice of Chicago culture. Street signs, posters, and sports memorabilia from the Windy City plaster the walls, and everyone in line yells a greeting to the owner in back swinging the spatula.

The menu reflects the best of Chi-Town: hot dogs, charbroiled sandwiches, wings, and burgers, including their version of the slider. Small burgers sizzle on a flattop griddle slathered with onions. They're served on a soft bun with a dab of brown mustard and ketchup. The first time I sat down with one I was skeptical. But that initial bite spun me into a culinary déjà vu. Not identical to White Castle but deliciously reminiscent, that same squishy collision of meat and onions floating in a cushioned bun. No wonder five hundred of the little darlings slide out the door daily. They cost about a buck and that's a small price to pay for a taste of home. 3749 E. Indian School Road, (602) 955-4137, www.chicagohamburger.com.

NO 22 North Trail, McDowell Mountains

If you feel intimidated by desert hiking, start with this trail. It's like venturing out with training wheels.

Flat, wide, and easy, North Trail wanders through a lovely corner of desert. Best of all, numbered markers dot the path identifying plants and landmarks. By the time you finish the gentle loop, you'll know much of the resident flora and how they survive and interact. Just grab a guide sheet at the visitor center before setting out and prepare to shake hands with the desert. Not literally, of course. Most everything out here will stab, jab, or claw you. The desert isn't cruel but neither does it abide carelessness.

The trail begins at a picnic area. Almost immediately you'll reach a junction where you'll turn right. McDowell Mountain Regional Park encompasses 21,099 acres of low desert plains and foothills. A lightning-sparked wildfire in 1995 savaged much of the park, but the area around North Trail was spared.

Hot Tip Fountain Hills is home to one of the world's tallest fountains. The fountain sprays water for about 15 minutes every hour and can reach a height of 560 feet.

The Sonoran is the most biologically diverse desert in North America with an incredible range of plants. You'll gain insight into this harsh but surprisingly fragile ecosystem courtesy of your trail guide. The only slight negative is that the markers have obviously been in place for a while. In some instances, the plants they had been identifying have since gone on to that big desert in the sky. So don't fret if you can't find everything advertised.

The trail never turns even vaguely challenging, although it does dip in and out of an occasional sandy wash. It's also popular with bikers, which I totally get. If I mountain biked, this would be the kind of route I would tackle, not those technical, ledged plunges where I usually find the lunatics. Park rangers often lead full-moon hikes on this trail, which must be devastatingly beautiful.

On the way back you'll enjoy views of some distant mountains including the Mazatzals and Superstitions. When you're ready for wilder, remoter desert, they're waiting for you.

Where: From Phoenix, take Loop 101 to Shea Boulevard. Exit and head east on Shea for 9 miles, turning left on Fountain Hills Boulevard. Continue traveling north, 7.5 miles as Fountain Hills becomes McDowell Mountain Park Drive. Turn left into McDowell Mountain Regional Park.

Wide, flat, and easy, North Trail is great desert hiking.

Cost: $6 per vehicle. **Difficulty:** Easy.
Length: 3.1-mile loop.
Details: (480) 471-0173,
www.maricopa.gov/parks/mcdowell.

Paradise Valley Burger Company
PHOENIX

Most food delivered in a plastic basket—and I speak with some authority here—isn't noted for its presentation. So I was pleasantly surprised at Paradise Valley Burger Company when my Beach House burger arrived looking like it was plated on fine china. A house-roasted poblano pepper draped the patty. A perfectly centered mound of smoked mozzarella balanced a pyramid of fresh pico de gallo that was piled tall as a toddler. I admired the artistry for about two seconds, then smooshed on the lid of the brioche bun and dove in.

The philosophy of Paradise Valley chef and owner Bret Shapiro is to keep things all about the food. The joint anchors one end of a strip mall and is totally nondescript. It's a stripped-down, no-frills business, which allows him to put everything in the basket. Outlandish gourmet burgers are served for a fraction of the price as upscale swanketerias. The ground chuck comes from a local meat

shop and is formed into a rustic, craggy patty. I like a rough-hewn burger that picks up a little char at the edges. Besides the Beach House, the other big seller is Burger Brûlée. Sugar burnt on the bun adds a sweet note while it holds the egg, bacon, and cheese together in a crunchy, yummy package. 4001 E. Bell Road, (602) 535-4930, www.pvburgercompany.com.

"I'll gladly pay you Tuesday for a hamburger today."

— J. WELLINGTON WIMPY

DESERT MOON

The moon and I go way back. We have a history. We've stayed up howling at each other many a night. I say without hesitation, there is no moon like a desert moon. When it climbs over the mountains all bright and bossy and fearless, it owns the sky. Stars are swept aside like dust specks and the Milky Way gets curdled. The moon flashes that diamond-toothed smile, the hard glitter that pulls tides from the sea, polishes cliffs to a glossy shine, and ties cactus spines in knots. Rivers bubbling below ground all day rise through the sand at the promise of a midnight kiss. Coyotes yip, kangaroo rats thump a bass line with big bony feet, and rattlesnakes form a percussion section shaking their tails till the dawn arrives and slaps some sense into them.

There is no moon like a desert moon.

DESERT ICON

Close your eyes and picture a cactus. Got one? Let me guess: Is it tall and straight with upraised arms? I thought so. The mighty saguaro is the quintessential cactus and the icon of the desert. And contrary to what you learn in western movies, they only grow in the Sonoran Desert. With the right conditions, saguaros can live to be 150 to 200 years old. They are a very slow-growing cactus, and the plant may only be an inch tall after their first decade. Arms normally begin to appear when the saguaro reaches 50 to 75 years of age. The saguaro is the largest cactus in the United States and can grow as high as a five-story building. They bloom from late April through early June. The saguaro blossom is the state flower of Arizona.

NO 23 Siphon Draw, Superstition Mountains

The Valley of the Sun sprawls across five hundred square miles, devouring desert and swarming over rocky slopes. Just when you think it will go on forever, a dark wall of mountains rise up, and civilization crashes and breaks like a wave against the steep ramparts. The Superstitions are the end of the world as we know it. Phoenix has rugged mountains in its midst but the Superstitions are another beast altogether, untamed and shrouded in legend.

The Siphon Draw Trail provides a good introduction to the Supes. The trail launches from the Saguaro Day-Use Area in Lost Dutchman State Park. At first it follows easy-peasy Discovery Trail, dotted with interpretive signs. Soon it turns onto an old mining road pointed toward the sheer-sided front range of the mountains. Other trails branch off at signed junctions but continue to plow ahead. As soon as it passes the Superstition Wilderness sign, the trail turns narrower and steeper.

If you've sworn off switchbacks, you're in luck because there's no weaving or winding here. It's a straight climb up the gullet of these hardscrabble mountains. Crazy, carved rock formations close around you as you approach the canyon. Glance to your right and see if you can pick out the Crying Dinosaur.

As the trail scrambled up a slickrock ledge, I stopped to look around. It was here I saw my first Gila monster years ago. Gila monsters are fat, venomous lizards covered with beadlike scales. They look like a poison purse. Despite a fearsome reputation, they're fairly sluggish and non-aggressive.

It was while jumping down from this ledge I suddenly saw the lizard directly below. He looked big enough to ride even without a saddle, but I thought it unwise. I managed to push off and cleared him by a couple of feet. He never even flicked a meaty tongue at me. When you're a burly steel-jawed sack of poison, nothing fazes you. I'm always thrilled to see wildlife so I studied him for a while (at a safe distance) before moving on. In my years of hiking, I've only seen one other Gila monster. They are a protected species, so treat them with

Siphon Draw Trail cuts into the rugged, mysterious Superstition Mountains.

respect, as you do all wildlife encountered. Do not harass, assault, or even heckle. We're guests in their house.

No sign of my old amigo as I continued my climb into the narrowing canyon where I reached a smooth basin of rock. After rains, the water cascades down the steep walls, filling this bowl.

Make this your turnaround spot. A sketchy and perilous pathway continues up to the top of Flatiron, the prominent outcrop high above, but it should only be attempted by experienced, hardcore, laugh-in the-face-of-danger hikers. On your return don't be embarrassed about butt-scooting down the water-polished rock. And keep an eye peeled for a beaded handbag in an unexpected place.

Where: Drive east from Phoenix on U.S. 60 to Apache Junction. Take exit 196, Idaho Road, north 5 miles to Arizona 88 and turn right. Continue on Arizona 88, Apache Trail, for another 5 miles and turn right into Lost Dutchman State Park.

Cost: Entrance fee is $7 per vehicle.

Difficulty: Moderate. **Length:** 4 miles round-trip.

Details: (480) 982-4485, www.azstateparks.com.

BOYCE THOMPSON ARBORETUM

Boyce Thompson Arboretum is Arizona's oldest and largest botanical garden. The 350-acre park was created to study drought-tolerant plants from around the world. Trails meander through diverse habitats such as herb gardens, cactus gardens, palm groves, and forests of shaggy-barked eucalyptus trees. Every few steps you'll stop to ponder how a collection of arid-friendly flora can appear so enchantingly lush. BTA is located on U.S. 60 at Milepost 223 about an hour's drive east of Phoenix. (520) 689-2811, www.azstateparks.com.

The Chuckbox   TEMPE

Gnarled and rickety, the Chuckbox is a burger shack sitting in the shadow of high-rises. Order a $\frac{1}{3}$- or $\frac{1}{2}$-pound patty and the grill man slaps it on the grate over a bed of mesquite charcoal. Orange flames shoot through the grill, charring patties, crisping bacon, and releasing a sizzling perfume. Beyond ingredients and recipes, a burger is a product of its environment, absorbing the memory of meat gone by, the ghost of ancient grease. This is the terroir of burgers. Each patty stands on the shoulders of burgers that came before. No seasoning compares to a well-used grill or griddle. Burgers at the Chuck are more than a sandwich; they're a beef vintage.

The simple menu offers burgers, garden burgers, and chicken sandwiches. Drag them through the well-stocked topping bar. I opt for mustard, chopped onions, and pickles—my ideal combo—with extra pickle slices for munching. It's a micro-salad I invented. Scattered tables fill the interior that seems as dark as Moe's Tavern. Tree stumps and wood crates serve as chairs. A sliver of patio lines one side of the shack. I sit there and dig in. I wonder if folks gazing out their high-rise windows can see how wide my grin is from such a distance. 202 E. University Drive, (480) 968-4712, www.thechuckbox.com.

THE LOST DUTCHMAN MINE

There are many versions of the tale of the Lost Dutchman Mine, but it usually goes like this: During the 1840s, the Peralta family of Mexico operated several mining claims, one being a rich gold mine in the Superstitions. An expedition returning ore to Mexico was attacked by Apaches and the miners perished.

Decades later, a Peralta descendant revealed the mine's location to Jacob Waltz, a German immigrant forever immortalized as the "Dutchman." Waltz worked the mine and killed anyone who happened by. On his deathbed in 1891, Waltz provided sketchy directions to friends caring for him. Thousands have searched for the fabled hole without success. Grisly murders and strange disappearances followed, cementing the sinister reputation of the Superstitions. Most geologists insist there is little geological evidence to suggest a rich gold deposit exists in these volcanic mountains.

NO 24 Vulture Peak, Wickenburg

You can see the clenched fist of Vulture Peak from all over Wickenburg. I'm no peak bagger but my first thought when I see a prominent mountain is to wonder if I can walk to the top. In this case the answer is yes, but barely.

The trail to the top of Vulture Peak offers three distinct segments. It starts out for the first 1.3 miles as a gentle meander through open desert, where teddy bear cholla grows so thick it looks like they were planted as a cash crop.

Fast Fact: During World War II, the U.S. Army trained thousands of men to be glider pilots at an airfield west of Wickenburg.

Views sweep away from the high saddle of Vulture Peak.

Saguaros are the kings of the cacti, tall and elegant with personality to spare as they poke holes in the sky. They always make me smile. But there's no reason to ignore the ground-level grunts, the blue-collar cacti like prickly pear, hedgehog, and cholla. They add a bristling back-story to the terrain on a daily basis and in springtime unfurl blooms in every shocking, scandalous hue imaginable.

Cactus flowers are so vivid because they take nothing for granted. All year long cacti bake in the sun, grabbing scant raindrops. Then for a week or so they shake off their gangster image and flash a softer side. Beneath the porcupine skin beats the heart of a poet.

The trail dips in and out of Syndicate Wash and crosses soft sloping desert to the base of the mountain. From here things get tougher. The second segment makes a steady climb, gaining seven hundred feet in a series of tight switchbacks that get steeper as you near a high saddle. The saddle appears as a notch in the long, gnawed ridgeline just below the summit.

Views from the saddle are expansive, so catch your breath and enjoy them. This makes a good turnaround point for all but the heartiest of hikers because the third segment of the trail is an ex-

tremely steep ascent to the summit. You'll scramble up through a narrow chute for the final 240 feet, portions of it a dizzying hand-over-hand climb. Those up to the challenge are rewarded by some lavish wraparound panoramas. It feels like you see most of central Arizona from this high perch.

Hot Tip The Lazy D Rockin' P Ranch operates horse-drawn carriage rides through downtown Wickenburg on Saturdays, October through April. They offer an overview of the area and lots of historic tidbits. (602) 316-1545, www.wickenburghorsecarriages.com.

Where: From Phoenix, take U.S. 60 West through Wickenburg. Turn left on Vulture Mine Road, which is the stoplight in front of Safeway. Drive approximately 6.5 miles to the Vulture Peak Trail turnoff. Follow the dirt road about a half-mile and park at the ramada. Four-wheel-drive vehicles may continue another 1.4 miles to the upper trailhead.

Cost: Free.

Difficulty: Strenuous.

Length: 4 miles round-trip.

Details: (623) 580-5500, www.blm.gov/az/st/en/prog/recreation/hiking/vulture.html

Chaparral Homemade Ice Cream

It was my dad who got me started on butter pecan ice cream when I was just a half-pint. I don't know why it resonated with me because it's a little subtle, a weird flavor for a kid. I grew up to be a raging chocoholic, yet if I had to pick a favorite scoop of ice cream, I'd cast my lot with butter pecan. So when I say the richest, nuttiest, most luscious butter pecan I ever had was at Chaparral, that's a pretty big deal. Then the owners, Tony and Pam Rovida, suggested that I try it as a sundae with hot fudge sauce. I had never even considered such a thing, but it was exquisite. Thank goodness I don't live in Wickenburg or I'd look like Jabba the Hutt.

For those who require more sustenance, they serve a full menu ranging from individual pizzas to crisp salads to hearty sandwiches. Everything at Chaparral is made from scratch, including the ice cream and luxurious, complex sauces that add extra zing to sundaes. Choose from 22 flavors with a monthly special. I won't bother to tell you what I'm ordering. 45 N. Tegner St., (928) 684-3252, www.chaparral-icecream.com.

HASSAYAMPA RIVER PRESERVE

For most of its 100-mile length, the Hassayampa River flows underground, but a geologic feature forces it to the surface for at least one portion. That riparian corridor

is now protected by the Nature Conservancy as the Hassayampa River Preserve. Three miles of trails loop beneath the shade of cottonwoods, willows, and California fan palms. Needless to say, the preserve is a birding hotspot and you're liable to catch sight of other wildlife, too. Word of warning: According to legend, anyone who drinks from the Hassayampa River never tells the truth again. 49614 U.S. 60, (928) 684-2772, www.nature.org/hassayampa.

SADDLE UP, DUDE

Wickenburg was once known as the "Dude Ranch Capital of the World" but only a few survive as travel tastes have changed. The Flying E welcomed their first guests in 1948. It's a traditional dude ranch where the focus is on horseback riding. They sit on 20,000 acres of scenic desert making for some epic trail rides. Ranch facilities also include a heated swimming pool, tennis courts, basketball court, and horseshoe pits. (888) 684-2650, www.flyingeranch.com.

Rancho de los Caballeros is more resort-oriented. Besides the riding, their championship golf course has been ranked as one of the top one hundred in the United States by *Golf Digest* and their luxury spa offers a range of treatments including a couples massage. Best of all, the ranch operates an extensive kids program, making this the best kind of family getaway, with something for everyone. (800) 684-5030, www.ranchodeloscaballeros.com.

NO 25 Wind Cave, Usery Mountains

The Usery Mountains rise along the eastern edge of the Phoenix metropolitan area, the beginning of a mountainous band that includes the Goldfields and the mighty Superstitions. At the geological heart of Usery Mountain Regional Park stands Pass Mountain. Craggy strata of volcanic rock earned the mountain its nickname "Scarface." High up that rocky cliff you'll find an unlikely little sanctuary known as the wind cave.

The trail rambles through a pretty patch of desert, rising only slightly at first. I'm surrounded by a gallery of desert denizens so profuse I expect to find a grounds keeping crew nooning in the shade of a palo verde tree. Strategically scattered boulders add a nice bit of texture to the usual suspects of saguaros, chollas, barrels, ocotillos, and creosote.

The only slight distraction is a muffled popping sound. Folks are firing off a few rounds at Usery Mountain Shooting Range. But it's far enough away so it just sounds like I've got some Orville Redenbacher in the microwave. Great. Now I'm craving popcorn.

Once the trail reaches the base of the mountain, it begins climbing in earnest, a steady grade of rocky switchbacks but never grueling. It is exposed the entire way with the sun just leaning on you. The desert can unleash a withering, angry heat, a heat that blowtorches the rocks and sand. It is a heat that will make you weep just so it can harvest your tears. So it is a great pleasure to reach your destination and slip out of the sun.

A scramble through pretty desert leads to the cool gash of Wind Cave.

Fast Fact: Usery Mountain was named for King Usery, a rancher from the area turned highwayman and horse thief. After his capture, he served time in Yuma Territorial Prison.

The cave is actually a scooped out alcove atop a ledge of lichen-covered volcanic tuff. It is a long swath of shade—lush sponge cake–like shade— with a cool breeze funneled through. The drop in temperature can be remarkable. Seeping water feeds bunches of rock daisies growing from the walls and ceiling. Bees swarm about, busy like always, but they pay me no mind. It's a sweet spot to relax and enjoy broad vistas across the valley floor.

Some adventurous types like to continue past the cave, climbing a rugged and unmaintained pathway to the top of Pass Mountain. You go ahead. I'll snooze here in the cool shade.

Where: From Phoenix, go east on U.S. 60 to Exit 191, Ellsworth Road. Head north on Ellsworth for 6.6 miles to Usery Mountain Regional Park.

Cost: $6 per vehicle.

Difficulty: Moderate.

Length: 3.2 miles round-trip.

Details: (480) 984-0032, www.maricopa.gov/parks/usery.

Flancer's   MESA

It all starts with the bread at Flancer's. They bake it fresh daily, sometimes a few times a day and that provides the foundation for the pizzas, sandwiches, and the burgers. Instead of buns they create long baguettes, soft but sturdy, sliced in a V-shape, which prompted a reinvention of the beef wheel. Instead of the classic circle, patties are formed into rectangles that nestle perfectly in the crusty crevice. It's a hamburger disguised as a hoagie. I didn't recognize it at first but before I could tell the waiter there's been a mistake, I caught that familiar aroma. That "bite me like you mean it" scent I know all too well.

The burger is crafted from an 80/20 blend of fresh ground chuck cooked to order on the flat-top. Along for the ride was a mound of lettuce, tomato, and red onion slices, plus a pickle spear to use as I saw fit. I quickly built a heaping sub that scored a direct hit on my taste buds. There are several side dishes to choose from including green chile mac and cheese. I stuck with fries because I'm a stodgy traditionalist who fears change. But I was not disappointed. They're batter coated with a nice crunchy texture. 1902 N. Higley Road, (480) 396-0077, www.flancers.com.

MADE IN THE SHADE

No one appreciates the subtle sweetness of shade like a desert dweller. Shade connects to the part of the brain trafficking in wonder and magic. Such a simple thing, yet one capable of delivering heart-freeing joy at the most opportune moments, shade infuses you with hope. Like pulling on pajamas that have been stored in the fridge, like being caught in a motionless rain, like tire-swinging into a farm pond, shade unfevers your brow. Shade is the breeze that doesn't brush past but instead cradles you, coos to you, says everything is going to be all right.

No one doubts the value of water in the desert. Water grabs all the good press, as if a horde of publicists work round the clock to enhance the image of H_2O. In the desert, water saves your life. Shade restores your faith.

DESERT BOTANICAL GARDEN

The Desert Botanical Garden in Phoenix is a spectacular landscape, veined by nature trails and bristling with over 20,000 desert plants from around the world. Set amidst the red rock buttes of Papago Park, the garden provides an exquisite introduction to the native plants and people of the desert regions. Indoor and outdoor exhibits and plenty of hands-on activities for the kids make this an excellent family outing. A café, garden shop, art gallery, and library are also on the property. 1201 N. Galvin Parkway, (480) 941-1225, www.dbg.org.

Fast Fact: Arizona has ninety wilderness areas, second only in number to California.

CHAPTER 7

TUCSON
AND THE
Southern Deserts

TUCSON ACTS AS ARIZONA'S CONSCIENCE. The town has sprawled in recent years, yet strives to preserve its multicultural heritage. Spanish, Mexican, and Native American influences are evident in the architecture, art, music, and cuisine of the community. That attitude of tolerance extends to the landscape. Ringed by mountain ranges and bookended by the two units of Saguaro National Park, Tucson doesn't battle the desert but rather embraces it. The Great Outdoors laps at residents' doorsteps, and everyone takes advantage. My hiking boots blend in nicely in the Old Pueblo, as Tucson is affectionately known.

The rest of Southern Arizona is an intoxicating blend of rugged scenery and Wild West history. Soaring mountains, harsh desert, and rolling grasslands define the frontier where a notorious cast of characters such as the Earps, the Clantons, Doc Holliday, and Johnny Ringo shot their way into the history books.

№ 26 Bear Canyon, Tucson

The official name may be Bear Canyon but nearly everyone calls it Seven Falls Trail because as improbable as it seems, a multi-terraced

~~~~~

A saguaro in the foothills of the Santa Catalina Mountains.

waterfall is your destination. Anytime you can find a seven-tiered waterfall in the desert, make the journey.

The trail leaves from Sabino Canyon Visitor Center. You can also take a shuttle into Bear Canyon for 1.5 miles, but didn't you come to hike? The trail starts off wide and flat and parallels the road with a few turns. Just follow Bear Canyon signs. Once the pavement ends, the footpath begins a gentle climb beside a stream that can turn feisty after a good storm. There are seven creek crossings on this section of trail entering the canyon.

One winter I was hiking here and it started raining hard. While the defile isn't narrow, it's never a good idea to be on a canyon floor with the potential for rising waters. I scrambled up a rocky wall and found an alcove to wait out the weather. Then an amazing thing happened. The rain vaporized and fog filled the canyon, wafting below me in tufted clouds. It was eerily quiet as I was engulfed in a glossy sheen of buttermilk and woodsmoke. For several minutes I couldn't see cactus, rock, or sky. Nothing existed beyond this swirling wispy wall of satin. It was not my typical desert hike.

After the last stream crossing, the trail clambers up the south canyon wall in a couple of languid switchbacks. You round a corner and see the falls slicing a sharp passageway down the cliff. The trail branches here with the left fork leading to the base of the falls and the right fork continuing deeper into Bear Canyon.

Hang a left and scramble down to the rocky cleft. The waterfall is seasonal, tumbling in terraced cascades, creating juicy little swimming holes at every level. The torrent is most pronounced in spring and after summer monsoons. But even when the falls are parched you'll find wide pools of clear water, a mirage-like oasis tucked away in the folds of the desert. It's like finding a sapphire in the couch cushions. Makes you wonder what other bits of magic lurk in the outback.

Where: From Tucson, take I-10 West to Ina Road Exit. Turn east on Ina Road and follow for 15.5 miles to a dead-end at Sabino Canyon Road. (Ina changes to Skyline and then to Sunrise but continue following the main road.) Turn left on Sabino Canyon and proceed to Sabino Canyon Recreation Area Visitor Center.

Cost: A $5 day pass is required.
Difficulty: Moderate.
Length: 8.2 miles round-trip.
Details: (520) 749-8700, www.fs.usda.gov/coronado.

The tumbling cascades of Seven Falls.

Hot Tip Fourth Avenue, an eclectic mix of boutiques, galleries, restaurants, and bars, borders the University of Arizona campus and is popular with students and residents. Live entertainment and street fairs break out at the drop of a hacky sack. (520) 624-5004, www.fourthavenue.org.

Pat's Drive-In   TUCSON

There's a siren song to this little fry-hole I can't resist. The shambling white building is hidden away in a Tucson working class neighborhood but it's also right off the interstate. I seldom drive past without stopping even if I'm on my way to dinner somewhere else, for crying out loud. These burgers are ridiculously addictive but they're small enough that I can justify them as appetizers.

Most of Pat's patrons aren't there for burgers. They come for the sloppy chili dogs and fresh-cut fries served in paper sacks. A few picnic tables provide seating indoors and out but it's mostly a drive-up, grab-'em-and-go kind of place. Pat's is so old school there's even a pay phone on the lot. (Kids unfamiliar with the term "pay phone," ask your parents. You won't believe it.) Burgers are slender patties topped with mustard, chopped onions, and lettuce. Decades fall away at each bite. These beauties taste like burgers grilled at lunch counters, pool halls, and five and dimes before the homogenization of America. These are burgers of a simpler time and place. They're the burgers of my youth. 1202 Niagara Street, (520) 624-0891.

TOHONO CHUL PARK

This 49-acre oasis offers visitors a quiet escape amid lush gardens, with beautiful views of the Santa Catalina Mountains. Stroll the winding paths through native flora

and don't be surprised if you're strafed by hummingbirds along the way. Spring wildflower displays are especially dazzling. Translated from the Tohono O'odham language, Tohono Chul means "desert corner." The park features cultural exhibits, a greenhouse, demonstration gardens, a children's garden, and a lovely tearoom that serves breakfast, lunch and, of course, afternoon tea. Park docents lead guided tours throughout the day. 7366 North Paseo Del Norte, (520) 742-6455, www.tohonochulpark.org.

TITAN MISSILE MUSEUM

Intriguing museums are scattered across Arizona but none is quite as haunting as the one just south of Tucson, where visitors climb into a silo to examine a Titan II missile on its launch pad. The Titan Missile Museum is the only U.S. nuclear-missile silo open to the public. Hour-long guided tours are offered daily, showing off the missile complex, launch center, 3-ton blast doors, and a close look at the largest nuke ever made in the United States. A simulated launch is conducted. The missile is unarmed, so you don't have to worry about your rambunctious youngster bumping a button and accidentally starting World War III. 1580 W. Duval Road, Sahuarita, (520) 625-7736, www.titanmissilemuseum.org.

N⁰ 27 Canyon Loop, Tucson

Catalina State Park covers 5,500 acres in the foothills of the Santa Catalina Mountains. And Canyon Loop dishes up some of the best the park has to offer in a short, easy-to-access package. From the trailhead, I cross the road and then the wash with a nice current of flowing water. You'll encounter four stream crossings along the loop but even when water is present, a moderate rock hop is usually all that's required to avoid wet feet.

There's a short climb from the creek to a meadow lined with mesquite and saguaro, framed by a dramatic backdrop of mountain views. I stumbled onto my favorite part of the hike a few hundred yards down the trail. On the right, at the path's edge, is a mesquite tree with a purple prickly pear cactus growing out of the trunk.

I've seen cacti growing out of rocks, upside down from ledge bottoms, and on the roofs of houses but seeing one three feet off the ground growing from a tree is a new one to me. I can never tell if cacti are fiercely determined or more laid back than Jeff

Canyon Loop Trail splashes across an occasionally wet but always lovely creek.

A triumph of saguaros along Canyon Loop Trail.

Sullivan's Eatery & Creamery

When you think ice cream parlor, you usually flash back to a '50s soda fountain. So you'd be off by a couple of decades at Sullivan's, which is more of a '70s family-style ice cream scoopery. It's a comfortable place and they are serious about their grub. Burgers are ground fresh daily at Dickman's Deli, just a few doors down in the same shopping plaza.

The one-third-pound patties are charbroiled to customer specs and served with sliced tomato, leaf lettuce, and pickle on a sesame seed bun. A range of toppings are available if you're so inclined. But don't overload the thing so you have no room for dessert. They often run specials pairing a burger, drink, and ice cream. Wait a sec . . . burger, drink, and ice cream? If I ever have a date with the gallows, I think I just came up with the menu for my last meal. 6444 N. Oracle Road, (520) 297-9974, www.sullivanseateryandcreamery.com.

Bridges in *The Big Lebowski*. Is this all part of some relentless drive to survive? Or maybe it's more like, "Dude, here's a thimbleful of dirt. Might as well sink some roots." Either way, this tree cactus is my new hero as it hitches a slow ride to the sky. Go, man, go!

Reaching the end of the meadow, the trail drops via a series of railroad tie–steps back to the wash. The second half of the trail follows the stream lined by sycamore, oak, and hackberry, with big saguaros ambling down the slope as if pondering a swim.

The Sutherland Trail enters from the right and is worth a short venture in the spring. According to park rangers, some of the best patches of wildflowers can be found not far down the Sutherland.

Back at the trailhead, there's a small, volunteer-run snack shop, which is a beautiful thing. Any time I can walk off a desert trail and score an ice cream sandwich before I even reach my truck is one of those small moments of joy that brightens my whole week.

Where: From Tucson, drive I-10 West toward Phoenix. Take Exit 240 (Tangerine Road). Turn right on Tangerine Road and proceed for 13 miles, turning right on E. Innovation Park Road. After a mile you'll see the park entrance on the left.

Cost: $7 per vehicle entrance fee.

Difficulty: Easy.

Length: 2.3 miles round-trip.

Details: (520) 628-5798, www.azstateparks.com.

COLOSSAL CAVE MOUNTAIN PARK

Colossal Cave has been shelter, shrine, hideout, and longtime tourist attraction. Around A.D. 900 the ancient Hohokam used the subterranean rooms for shelter, food storage, and as a site of religious ceremonies. In 1887, bandits hid out in the cave in between train robberies. This also prompted the legend that sacks of loot are still stashed somewhere in a dark crevice. Tours started in the 1920s and continue today into the deep, hollow mountain. Sadly, damage was done to some formations in the early days of tourism, but this big three-dimensional maze still offers plenty of intriguing geological features. Other ways to explore Colossal Cave include Ladder Tours, Candlelight Tours, and Wild Cave Tours. 16721 E. Old Spanish Trail, Vail, (520) 647-7275, www.colossalcave.com.

Along the Way...

MINI-TIME MACHINE MUSEUM OF MINIATURES

It's not only a small world but an adorably small one at this charmingly quirky museum. Actually, it's several worlds. Designed as a time machine to transport visitors to different lands and times, the modernistic building overflows with all things wee, spread throughout themed rooms. The collection includes over two hundred houses and room boxes, including one of the oldest miniature displays (circa 1775) in the country. 4455 E. Camp Lowell Dr., (520) 881-0606, www.theminitimemachine.org.

OLD TUCSON STUDIOS

Fans of western movies might stop to genuflect in the dusty streets where the likes of John Wayne and Clint Eastwood once squinted. Dozens of movies have been filmed here over the years, including genuine classics and my all-time favorite, *Rio Bravo*. After a 1995 fire destroyed much of the studio, it was rebuilt into more of a theme park with museums, historian-led tours, and western-themed rides. There's still plenty of gunplay on the streets of Old Tucson as elaborately choreographed gunfights and stunt shows entertain visitors throughout the day. There's also a cancan musical in the saloon and a snake oil salesman peddling his wares. (520) 883-0100, www.oldtucson.com.

ARIZONA-SONORA DESERT MUSEUM

In a perfect world, all zoos would look like the Arizona-Sonora Desert Museum. It's a combination botanical garden, natural history museum, and zoo, with natural enclosures sheltering the animals. It's the next best thing to seeing them in the wild. Nearly two miles of hiking trails weave among the cacti and put you almost face to face with the critters. The riparian corridor offers aboveground and underwater viewing areas. Watching the river otters frolic is alone worth the price of admission. 2021 N. Kinney Road, (520) 883-2702, www.desertmuseum.org.

O.K. CORRAL

When it comes to Wild West history, Arizona takes a back seat to no one. And Tombstone serves as ground zero for that violent past. Gunfight reenactments occur daily at the O.K. Corral. These are full-blown theatrical productions of the famed shootout ending with a flourish of well-staged carnage. As part of the admission, visitors can tour C. S. Fly's historic photography studio, a cowboy bunkhouse, and a brothel. Before leaving, don't miss the Historama, a sweetly clunky multi-media show from 1963 narrated by the least cowboy-like star available at the time, Vincent Price. 326 E. Allen Street, (520) 457-3456, www.okcorral.com.

Hugh Norris chases a high ridgeline toward Wasson Peak.

NO 28 Hugh Norris, Tucson

Unlike some summit hikes that become head-bowed, foot-plodding slogs, the Hugh Norris Trail qualifies as an airy jaunt that keeps your noggin on a swivel while you gawk at one sweeping view after another. There are a few moderately steep pitches but that only sweetens the deal. It makes you feel like you earn the expansive vistas, among the best in Tucson in my opinion.

Set in Saguaro National Park West, the trail carves a route through classic Sonoran landscape to the top of 4,687-foot-high Wasson Peak, highest point in the Tucson Mountains. Named for a Tohono O'odham police chief, the trail starts out on a cactus-studded bajada as it switchbacks upward to snag a rocky ridgeline. From there the trail angles toward Wasson, hugging first one side of the high shoulder and then the other, alternating the views.

A coffee klatch of saguaros crowds the slopes along with assorted barrels, chollas, and ocotillos. You'll pass evidence of mining activity, including fenced-off shafts, and at the three-mile point you'll reach the junction of the Sendero Esperanza Trail.

Hot Tip The sun doesn't just set in Tucson; it swoons, collapsing like a blood orange in a flaming lemon glaze. The high perch of Gates Pass provides a front-row seat to the daily drama. Arrive an hour before sunset to snag a parking space. Drive west on Speedway Boulevard (which becomes Gates Pass Road) to the apex.

From here you're navigating a gauntlet of panoramas that surround the ridge top. This stretch is easy walking until one last twisted spiral of steep switchbacks deposits you on Wasson Peak. Don't expect a comforting forest canopy atop the high slopes. The Tucsons never gain enough elevation to shake off the heat and cacti. It's a desert hike bottom to top and shade is as thin and unreliable as an undertaker's smile. I sit atop the summit, a rocky knob with wraparound views, as the sun pokes a spicy finger in my chest.

This is an elegant landscape, all stone and spine,

lumbering mountains, and belligerent light. In the clear stillness I can hear the desert growling at me. Or maybe purring. Either way, I'm good.

Where: Trail begins in the Tucson Mountain District of Saguaro National Park. From Tucson, drive west on Speedway, which becomes Gates Pass Road, until it dead ends at Kinney Road. Turn right on Kinney and proceed 4.7 miles to the visitor center.

Cost: Entrance fee is $10. **Difficulty:** Moderate. **Length:** 9.8 miles round-trip.
Details: (520) 733-5183, www.nps.gov/sagu.

El Güero Canelo

TUCSON

I rue the day I ate my first Sonoran hot dog because it is one of those specific and persistent cravings that can't be satisfied by anything else. The Sonoran hot dog is the saguaro cactus of wieners. It is the closest thing Arizona has to an official hot dog. The messy concoction is a treasure trove of flavors but the essence is the bacon-wrapped hot dog. And for the record, "bacon-wrapped" may very well be the most wonderful hyphenate ever created. Opened in 1993, El Güero Canelo was one of the first to introduce Sonoran dogs to the Tucson market.

The dog is a special kind of sin, swaddled in bacon and grilled, fusing the meats into a smoky flavor bomb. It is then tucked into a soft boat of a bun, fluffier than the traditional bolillo. Keeping the dog company are whole pinto beans, diced tomatoes, grilled and fresh onions, mustard, mayo, and jalapeño sauce. You can wash it down with Coca-Cola bottled in Mexico and made with real cane sugar. El Güero Canelo has multiple Tucson locations but I usually visit the one on Oracle. 2480 N. Oracle Road, (520) 882-8977, www.elguerocanelo.com.

Fast Fact: Mount Lemmon, in the Santa Catalina Mountains, is home to the southernmost ski resort in the United States.

NO 29 Cochise Trail, Sunsites

The Dragoons are a delicious clutter of mountains. They are a sudden idea of stone, a whim of granite rising abruptly from shaggy grasslands in southeastern Arizona.

Cochise Stronghold in the Dragoon Mountains once provided refuge to the legendary Apache chief, Cochise. The Dragoons form both maze and natural fortress amid a jumble of boulders and angular cliffs. In the mountains, Cochise and his followers could find food, medicine, and year-round water. And from the high vantage point, the Apaches had excellent views of the valleys on either side. They could literally see the army coming two days before it arrived.

Jumbled boulder fields line Cochise Trail.

One of my great regrets is that I'm not hiking here every month, spending more time exploring these granite spires and slashing chasms. Some mountains soar, but the Dragoons seem to roll over the landscape. For thirty miles the Dragoons—surging, falling, cresting, and curling—appear as if a pounding surf had somehow turned to stone during high tide.

Starting in the Cochise Stronghold Campground, the Cochise Trail branches off from an interpretive nature loop, which is a nice bonus. The signs along the way introduce you to native plants and their uses to the Apache people.

For the first mile, the trail weaves through the lush canyon bottom, dotted with manzanita, beargrass, and yuccas. Clustered boulders frequently interrupt the dense screen of vegetation. After a

Crumpled granite columns stand guard over Halfmoon Tank.

few moderate switchbacks, I arrive at Halfmoon Tank. This dammed stock pond supports a small riparian community ringed by granite pinnacles.

Three miles into the hike, I reach the saddle that marks Stronghold Divide. There is a piñon pine here that I greet like an old friend. Beneath the shady canopy is one of my favorite trail snooze spots. And while I don't want to boast, I am a master of the trail snooze. A quick nap sprawled on boulders, across tree roots, on high rock ledges—it doesn't matter. I can doze anywhere outdoors and wake feeling refreshed. There's something about the combination of weariness and shade plus the joy sloshing around in my heart that proves conducive to a little shuteye. It feels like an angel sucker punches me as I tumble suddenly but gently into dreamland.

Beyond the divide, the trail drops steeply into the Stronghold Canyon West. Most people use the divide as a turnaround point, but I push on because I love this next portion. There's a geological belligerence to the western defile. The rock-crowned cliffs and bald domes become more pronounced. The Dragoons have a shape-shifting character, absorbing light, throwing shadows, and changing colors throughout the day. Turn the Grand Canyon inside out and you have the Dragoons.

The western half of the trail ends at a 4WD road in a woodland of oak and juniper. Of course, upon reaching this point, I have to turn around and make the steep climb back out. This is where the benefits of the trail snooze pay off in spades. I'm over the saddle and back at the trailhead in no time flat.

Where: From Tucson, take I-10 east 72 miles to U.S. 191. Turn south and drive 17.5 miles to Ironwood Road. Turn right and drive 9.2 miles to Cochise Stronghold Campground. Portions of Ironwood Road are graded dirt but suitable for all vehicles. Trail begins on the east end of campground, across a wooden bridge.

Cost: Free. **Difficulty:** Moderate.

Length: 10 miles round-trip.

Details: (520) 364-3468, www.fs.usda.gov/coronado.

Fast Fact: Hostilities between Cochise and the U.S. military began following the "Bascom Affair." In 1861, Army Lt. George Bascom wrongly accused Cochise of kidnapping a child and tried to hold the Apache chief captive. Although Cochise escaped, several of his family members were held and later executed. What followed were eleven years of bloody warfare on the Arizona frontier.

Horseshoe Café & Bakery

BENSON

As you can guess from the name, a cowboy motif gallops through this historic café. A giant neon horseshoe adorning the ceiling, local brands burned into wooden posts, and murals painted by western artist Vern Parker are all part of the decor. The Horseshoe has been a Benson institution since 1936. The menu includes such old-fashioned dishes as liver and onions, meatloaf, bone-in pork chops, and chicken-fried steak.

The slate of charbroiled half-pound burgers includes one piled with pastrami and another stuffed with bleu cheese. The Horseshoe Signature Burger comes topped with cream cheese and pickled jalapeño slices and served with lettuce, tomato, pickles, and a big slice of onion. I haven't tried that one yet, preferring to stick to beefy basics. You're given plenty of options for sides and it may be wise to venture beyond the fries, which are fairly pedestrian. Be sure to save room for something sweet. The dessert case by the front door is jam-packed with homemade cakes, pies, and pastries. 154 E. 4th Street, (520) 586-2872.

NO 30 Heart of Rocks, Chiricahua National Monument

Tucked away in the southeastern corner of the state, the 12,000-acre national monument shelters an exotic array of sculpted stone. Massive columns, slender spires, and impossibly balanced boulders loom above the timber. The skyline seems built from the splintered remains of ancient castles.

About 27 million years ago a savage volcanic event lashed this corner of the world. The eruption, a thousand times more powerful than Mount St. Helens, spewed ash and pumice over 1,200 square miles. The mixture cooled and fused into a tuff of rhyolite. A few eons of erosion carved the welded rhyolite into an enchanting forest of formations. The Chiricahua Apaches called these mountains the "Land of Standing Up Rocks." Walking among the volcanic stubble, I am always mesmerized by one of the most brain-spraining spots in Arizona.

An interconnected network of trails provides Chiricahua visitors with several hiking options. The short loop through Heart of Rocks is the craggy core of the park, where you'll find the most spectacular collection of formations. The easiest route to Heart of Rocks is via a trio of trails: Ed Riggs (0.9 miles), Mushroom Rock (1.2 miles), and Big Balanced Rock (1 mile). From Echo Canyon parking lot, start on Ed Riggs, which drops gradually into a finger canyon bracketed by fractured columns and thrusts of stone. The trail ends at a three-way junction. Jump on the Mushroom Rock Trail. You'll spot Mushroom Rock in a quarter-mile above the trees

LARIAN MOTEL

There's no better bargain in Tombstone than the Larian Motel. Rooms are just retro enough to stir up memories of family road trips from your youth, yet all the amenities are decidedly modern. Plush beds, free Wi-Fi, and mini-fridges are just a few of the creature comforts. Rooms are spacious and immaculate. Plus, the Larian sits smack in the middle of the historic district so everything is just footsteps from your door. 410 E. Fremont Street, (520) 457-2272, www.tombstonemotels.com.

A chorus of rhyolite columns on the trail to Heart of Rocks.

on your right. If you're slightly underwhelmed by the flattop fungus of stone, don't sweat it. Lots more dramatic formations are ahead.

The trail climbs through a forested ravine where it connects with Big Balanced Rock Trail. The burn scars you see here and elsewhere along the trails are the result of a 2011 fire. Big Balanced Rock follows a high ridgeline with sweeping views. Look for Cochise Head, a striking mountain that suggests the noble profile of Cochise. Soon you pass through a corridor of stacked rocks and haunting hoodoos. Near the end of the trail, you'll spot the namesake 1,000-ton boulder perched on a thumb of stone. From here a short spur trail leads to Heart of Rocks.

Take the 1.1-mile loop clockwise, which affords better views of the weird stone garden. Volcanic intensity still crackles within this twisty little laby-rinth, undercut by a sneaky sense of whimsy. You're surrounded by tumbled, crumpled, otherworldly rock formations, like somebody busted up Stone-henge and the Easter Island heads for kindling.

From the chaos looms the familiar as you wind through the forest. Unexpected shapes suddenly burst into sight. Behold, Thor's Hammer! Hey, a Duck on a Rock! Visions of Punch and Judy, Camel's Head, and the Totem Pole pull you along. I love the weird verticality of this place where the rocks seem so alert, so poised. There's an air of expectancy here as if they could go marching down the mountain at any moment and are just waiting for a signal.

Reconnect with Big Balanced Rock Trail and the return is mostly downhill to the trailhead, always a nice way to end a hike.

Where: Chiricahua National Monument is located 120 miles southeast of Tucson. From I-10 East take Exit 340 in Willcox. Drive south on Arizona 186 for 32 miles to the junction of Arizona 181. Turn left and proceed 4 miles to the park.

Cost: $5 per person.

Difficulty: Moderate.

Length: 7.3 miles round-trip.

Details: (520) 824-3560, www.nps.gov/chir.

BISBEE

The bright yellow building on the south side of Bisbee started as a hot dog stand, as evidenced by the giant wiener mounted on the roof. But owner Jimmy Pionke, a big loveable palooka from Chicago, expanded the menu, keeping things simple but delicious. The man has a Midas touch in the kitchen. His burgers are divine, his pulled pork smoky and tender, and his fries may be the best I have ever had. Five minutes before you're gobbling them, they were a potato.

The signature dish at Jimmy's remains the classic Chicago hot dog, which is culinary architecture. To qualify as a Chicago dog, an exacting blueprint must be followed. Start with the Cadillac of tube steak, Vienna all-beef hot dogs in natural casings. The casing gives it that satisfying snap, releasing juices and flavor at every bite. The dog nestles on a poppy seed bun. Ingredients are piled on in precise order—mustard, neon green relish, chopped onions, tomato wedges, a pickle spear, two sport peppers, and a dash of celery salt. The result is a private riot in your mouth, a joyous collision of flavors. Jimmy's serves a full slate of dogs and sandwiches and they all come with fresh-made fries, bursting with an earthy zing of real potato taste. 938 W. Arizona 92, (520) 432-5911.

Fast Fact: The Chiricahua Mountains are one of the "sky islands" of Southern Arizona. Sky islands are forest-clad mountain ranges isolated from one another by expansive valleys of grasslands or desert.

ARIZONA FOLKLORE PRESERVE

The Arizona Folklore Preserve, nestled in Ramsey Canyon near Sierra Vista, is an intimate state-of-the-art theater that seats sixty, putting the audience practically on stage with the entertainers. It was founded by Dolan Ellis, Arizona's Official State Balladeer, so performers could celebrate our western heritage and help preserve local folk songs, stories, and legends. Ellis, who was an original member of the New Christy Minstrels, remains artist-in-residence. He performs one weekend each month and his shows are a riveting, joyous lesson in Arizona history and lore. (520) 378-6165, www.arizonafolklore.com.

BISBEE

Allow yourself plenty of time to poke around in Bisbee, a former mining town turned funky artist community. The little hamlet appears to be spackled into the nooks and crannies of the Mule Mountains. Clusters of houses zigzag up cliff faces, defying gravity and common sense. Others flow in and out of gulches and spill over ledges. Narrow streets curl into the hills and vanish. Some houses can only be reached by stairs. Some stairs can only be reached by other stairs. Think of the least likely spot imaginable to build a town. Got it? Welcome to Bisbee, San Francisco's little slacker cousin. (520) 432-5421, www.bisbeearizona.com.

"Everywhere is walking distance if you have the time."

—STEVEN WRIGHT

Tumacácori National Historic Park caught in the failing light of late day.

NO 31 Juan Bautista de Anza Trail, Tubac

Water drastically changes the desert equation and nowhere is that more evident than in the Santa Cruz River Valley. Driving south from Tucson, the desert doesn't turn spinier as you might expect; instead it softens, becomes downright pastoral. Cactus-dotted slopes give way to rolling grasslands, shaggy with mesquite.

The Juan Anza Trail is not your typical desert hike but that's what makes it so special. The trail connects Tumacácori National Historic Park to Tubac Presidio State Historic Park via a riparian corridor rich with history. In 1775, Spaniard Juan Bautista de Anza led more than 240 colonists to California where they founded the city of San Francisco. This is part of the trail they took.

> **Hot Tip** 〰 The Village of Tubac is a shopaholic's dream destination, with over one hundred art galleries and gift shops packed into a few scenic blocks. The Village is open year round, but winter is the busiest time. Many shop owners close during the summer, a missed opportunity because summer evenings in the Santa Cruz Valley are ripe and luscious.

The pathway follows the Santa Cruz River, which flows north, unlike most rivers that run south. It weaves its way through a shady mesquite bosque. The walking is easy across level terrain and over soft, sandy soil. Footbridges solve the river crossings and posts marked by the Anza Trail logo keep you pointed in the right direction. Built by volunteers at the Anza Trail Coalition, this is a

Juan Anza Trail.

popular spot for birding. I always intend to learn to identify more birds but never get around to it. I am better at quietly following knowledgeable birders and eavesdropping on their sightings.

The trail ends at the Tubac Presidio, which was designated as Arizona's first state park in 1958. It preserves the heritage and ruins of the first European settlement in what would become Arizona. Tubac was established as a Spanish presidio (fort) in 1752. Those early ruins are still visible in an underground exhibit. Visitors will also see an impressive museum that houses Arizona's first printing press with demonstrations, a furnished 1885 schoolhouse, and living history exhibits.

This trail is a simple woodland stroll along an intermittent river. But spending time at the weathered yet elegant Tumacácori mission church and the Tubac Presidio to discover the area's rich history makes this a most memorable experience.

Where: From Tucson, go south on I-19 to Exit 29. Drive north on East Frontage Road, 0.7 miles to Tumacácori National Historic Park. The trailhead is located just north of the visitor center parking lot, directly across from the post office.

Cost: Free to hike the trail. There are modest

Fast Fact: In 1691, Father Eusebio Francisco Kino established Tumacácori as one of the first Spanish missions in what would become Arizona.

admission fees for Tumacácori National Historic Park and Tubac Presidio State Historic Park.

Difficulty: Easy.

Length: 9 miles round-trip.

Details: (520) 398-2341, www.nps.gov/tuma.

Wisdom's Café

TUMACÁCORI

The Wisdom family has been welcoming neighbors and tourists alike to their homey eatery for a few generations now, dating back to 1944. Wisdom's Café sits a half mile north of Tumacácori with giant fiberglass chickens standing guard. They're well known for hearty chimichangas, shredded beef or turkey, as well as their Mason jar margaritas. And that big half-pound burger isn't on the menu just for show; it's quite tasty.

You can start with a giant cheese crisp, always a good appetizer choice. But no matter how you begin, finish with a fruit burrito. A hot flour tortilla stuffed with fruit filling, dusted with cinnamon and sugar, is served à la mode and should not be missed. 1931 E. Frontage Road, (520) 398-2397, www.wisdomscafe.com.

SAY CHEESE!

If you're not from Arizona, you probably never heard of a cheese crisp. I weep for all you have missed. No food I can think of is as simple yet so devastatingly delicious. A flour tortilla swabbed with a little butter, covered in shredded cheese and baked at volcanically high temperatures until crisp. Fancy it up with onions or green chile strips if you want but really nothing else is needed. Served open face, usually as an appetizer, it's a big plate of ooey, gooey, cheesy goodness.

The cheese crisp is a menu mainstay in Arizona but rarely found outside the state. Tortillas big as tire rims draped in cheese are meant to be shared. But if you plan on splitting one with me, better bring your Sunday teeth. I work fast. They should be eaten hot, and I refuse to sit idly by letting cheesy slices cool and congeal just because you're feeling blabby. All politeness ends at the charred edge of a cheese crisp.

TUBAC GOLF RESORT & SPA

Tubac Golf Resort & Spa occupies part of the historic Otero cattle ranch. Bing Crosby and cronies bought the ranch in 1959 and started the golf resort. Original buildings have been incorporated into the elegant design, and the resort embraces its ranching heritage. Cattle grazing in the rough can add an extra challenge to golfers. (The course was also the setting for the movie *Tin Cup*.) Luxury haciendas each feature beautiful tile work, sunken living room, flat screen TV, walk-in shower, fireplace, and patio. Views stretch across the lush greens to the cottonwood-draped river to the mountains beyond. (800) 848-7893, www.tubacgolfresort.com.

CHAPTER

№ 8

ARIZONA'S
West Coast

OF ALL THE UNEXPECTED SIGHTS in Arizona—and the state is lousy with them—the West Coast may be the most freakishly refreshing. The Colorado River defines the western edge of Arizona and creates an authentic, albeit slender, coastline. But push back from the water even a tiny bit and you run smack into serious desert.

Instead of the familiar and relatively verdant Sonoran Desert, a sliver of the Mojave muscles in. The majestic saguaros are replaced by the twisted, haunted shapes of Joshua trees. Spindly creosote bushes dot the landscape. Amid this rock-strewn, sun-chewed terrain, you'll find an abundance of places to explore.

№32 Crack-in-the-Mountain, Lake Havasu City

Lake Havasu City serves as the central hub of a splashy playground. And while nearly everyone goes for the water, landlubbers like me dig their unsung network of trails. Crack-in-the-Mountain for example, sends you slithering through a winding slot canyon near the banks of the mighty Colorado. Start out on a wide path from the parking area following the yellow trail markers. You

Views of raw and rugged Mojave Desert from Telegraph Pass.

soon drop into a sandy wash. Just past the one-mile mark, the wash bends to the left and stone walls rise up to greet you. As you enter the canyon, there's a small triangle-shaped arch on your left that is virtually impossible to see head on. Glance back before the narrows and you'll spot it.

The slot canyon runs through a banded rhyolite lava flow. The flow bands indicate the dynamics of the lava as it moved downslope from its vent and are preserved like swirls in marbled ice cream. The pearl-smooth walls are only a few feet apart through the heart of the narrows as you wind your way through the stone-wrapped tunnel. There's a seven-foot dry waterfall perfect for sliding down. There's usually a rope anchored to the rock, providing assistance to non-sliders.

Fast Fact: Lake Havasu is ringed by over twenty lighthouses. They're designed as 1/3-scale replicas of famous lighthouses and serve as navigational beacons for boaters. They've also become popular tourist attractions.

Everyone should spend time in a slot canyon. With boots on the ground and a hand on each wall, you connect to the landscape in a way you never do elsewhere. It is restorative. Slot canyons impart long forgotten life lessons, stuff we knew when we were six but lost sight of. Tight spaces are meant to be squeezed through. Focus on small things. Slide at every opportunity. The world can be big and overwhelming at times, so you should always have a good hideout.

The canyon widens out at 1.4 miles. You can turn around and return through the Crack or climb a short (but slightly steep) pathway up the right bank to the Blue Trail that follows the ridge-line back. Or continue down the wash (angling to the right when vegetation blocks the path) to the banks of the Colorado River. You reach a quiet cove near Balanced Rock. From here, climb the ridge and return via the Blue Trail.

Canyon walls pinch the trail down to a sliver.

Where: Trailhead is in SARA Park, six miles south of London Bridge. From downtown Lake Havasu City, drive south on U.S. 95 to S. McCulloch Boulevard at Milepost 177. Turn right and travel 0.7 miles to the parking lot on the right.

Cost: Free.

Difficulty: Moderate.

Length: 2.8 miles round-trip through the Crack and back; 5 miles round-trip if you go to the Colorado River.

Hikers squeeze through the slot canyon known as Crack-in-the-Mountain.

Details: (800) 242-8278, www.golakehavasu.com.

Sandbar & Grill

LAKE HAVASU CITY

Glancing around the Sandbar, I realize I'm the only one wearing socks. I'm also one of the few wearing shoes and a shirt. It's a rare day when I'm the most overdressed person in a crowd, but beach rules apply at the Sandbar. I walked off the trail, but everyone else strolled over from a boat or beach towel. Swim trunks and bikinis are the attire du jour. Sandbar is a seasonal burger stand sitting at the water's edge. They're closed during winter months and seating is all outdoors. Order at the counter where the menu is scrawled in Sharpie across a surfboard.

They've got several burgers to choose from and they go down fast and easy. The hand-formed patties have some heft. Mine comes with a big ripe tomato, fresh leaf lettuce, pickles, and a lightly toasted bun. I was admir-ing a curvaceous blonde wearing three paint swatches as a bathing suit but forgot all about her as soon as my burger arrived. I chomped through it in nothing flat while pondering what an impossible ending this was to the day. I'm eating a burger on the beach, watching a flotilla of boats spread across the water. And I never left Arizona. 1340 McCulloch Boulevard N., (928) 854-7263.

Jersey's Grill
LAKE HAVASU CITY

Sitting in the shadow of London Bridge, this is Lake Havasu City's quasi-official patio. A dozen yellow picnic tables under a bright yellow roof make the place hard to miss. And you certainly shouldn't. Pull up a hunk of pine and enjoy a charbroiled burger or authentic Philly cheesesteak while gazing on the authentic London Bridge. The bridge, which spanned the River Thames from the 1830s, was purchased by Robert McCulloch, founder of Lake Havasu City. It was packed up and reconstructed in the Arizona desert. Since 1971, it has crossed the Bridgewater Channel and Jersey's Grill provides a front row seat.

Their specialty burgers are made with fresh-ground chuck, several of them big, sloppy elbow-drippers. The Memphis comes topped with scratch-made barbecue sauce, bacon, and a heaping portion of coleslaw. You can even score one topped with their Philly steak meat. They have a second location downtown if you ever feel the urge to go inside. 401 English Village, (928) 854-3938, www.jerseysgrilllakehavasu.com.

"Part of the secret of a success in life is to eat what you like and let the food fight it out inside."

—MARK TWAIN

N⁰ 33 Monolith Garden Trail, Kingman

Kingman definitely keeps its hiking bounty on the down-low. The town has constructed a beautiful network of trails slashing across the Cerbat Foothills Recreation Area but doesn't do much to promote them. The Monolith Garden Trail is my favorite, a tangled route through dramatic boulder fields and crumbling ramparts of volcanic ash.

Three different trailheads and multiple forks make Monolith Gardens a bit of a maze. It's sort of a loop within a loop. I start from the Metwell trailhead and cut across rocky hills dotted with ocotillo and crucifixion thorn. Soon after passing through a gate, I reach the loop portion, which I take clockwise.

I pass two junctions branching off to the right, each with a generic trail marker. These can be used if you prefer making a shorter loop. But unless I'm limping, I don't believe in shorter loops. I continue straight ahead where I'm soon skirting the edge of a small canyon with scalloped rock walls.

The Mojave is a more languid desert than the Sonoran. Vegetation is more haphazard and it lacks the vertical notes of the saguaro. I love how quickly this trail cuts you free. U.S. 93 is the highway to Las Vegas, so there's a nearby stream of high-rollers anxious to be hand-fed a shrimp cocktail by an Elvis impersonator while soaking in a hot tub filled with absinthe, or whatever the popular trend is in Sin City. But I'm winding through open country detached from it all.

A pretty hike, Monolith Garden is also a great name for a trail.

Unexpected formations loom along Monolith Garden Trail.

The trail continues through a rolling landscape of low slanted hills, past stacked rock towers and hunched ridgelines toothy with columns. As I'm swinging back around, I ignore a couple of unmarked trails entering from the left. Then I pass the other loop trails coming in from the right. At the third trail junction, I hang a right even though the path continues straight ahead. I continue on this segment, despite yet another turnoff with a TH marker. I finally reach my familiar junction and turn back toward my truck.

It's probably a good idea to stop by the Kingman Visitor Center or the Bureau of Land Management Office and grab a map. I figured it out on my own but why put yourself through needless worry? It's a dandy trail but not much shade. Carry plenty of water.

Where: The easiest trailhead to access is on Metwell Drive. From I-40, turn north on U.S. 93 (Exit 48). Turn left on Metwell, approximately a half mile from the interstate. Proceed 0.1 miles to a dirt road. Turn right to trailhead.

Cost: Free.

Difficulty: Moderate.

Length: 8 miles.

Details: (928) 718-3700, www.blm.gov/az/st/en/prog/recreation/hiking/monolith.html.

Fast Fact: Over 90 percent of leafy vegetables consumed in the United States from November through March are produced in Yuma.

Redneck's Southern Pit Barbecue

KINGMAN

Even though I'm a hardcore burger guy, here's my theory: If you arrive in a strange town and know nothing about local restaurants, eat at a barbecue place. People don't open a barbecue joint as part of some business plan. They do it because they've been barbequing all their lives. They have a passion for making food "low and slow." It's in their very marrow. People learn to cook for others but they barbecue for themselves.

For years Bubba and Tammy Floyd served their down-home pulled pork, slow-cooked ribs, and hearty side dishes at Mohave County events. So when the Floyds opened a cozy eatery in 2009, crowds poured in, hungry for more. Redneck's specializes in meaty racks of St. Louis–style ribs that are tender but not helpless. They offer just a hint of resistance, refusing to surrender without a bite. That texture makes them all the more delicious. All meats are cooked over hickory wood fires. But no matter how tasty the meal, save room for pie. The Ulti-

mate Frozen Lemon Pie is a towering stack of creamy lemon goodness that arrives like plated sunshine. If it's not my favorite pie of all time, it's in contention. Try it; you'll thank me later. 420 E. Beale Street, (928) 757-8227, www.reodneckssouthernpitbbq.com.

Along the Way...

BILL WILLIAMS RIVER
NATIONAL WILDLIFE REFUGE

South of Lake Havasu, Bill Williams River carves a verdant slash across an otherwise forbidding landscape, soothing the sun-scarred crossroads where the Sonoran and Mojave deserts collide. Established in 1941 to protect this vital waterway, the Bill Williams River National Wildlife Refuge covers 6,105 acres and stretches from the marshy confluence at Lake Havasu back through the lush valley. The refuge contains one of the last stands of cottonwoods and willows that can be found on the Colorado River, providing essential habitat for a variety of wildlife.

Over 350 species of birds have been identified in the refuge, including the endangered Yuma clapper rail and the southwestern willow flycatcher. The refuge supports forty species of butterflies and fifty-seven species of mammals including desert bighorn sheep and an occasional mountain lion. (928) 667-4144, www.fws.gov/refuge/bill_williams_river.

CHLORIDE

Arizona is blessed with loads of quirky towns sprouting in the middle of nowhere, but none top Chloride for distinctive personality. Curled at the foot of the Cerbat Mountains eighteen miles north of Kingman, Chloride is a former mining town best known for 2,000 square feet of gloriously garish murals splashed across granite boulders. Internationally known artist Roy Purcell first painted the "The Journey" in 1966 and then repainted it at the town's invitation in 2006. That same artistic passion can be found in the handful of galleries and the wide-ranging displays of yard art that fill the town. Gunfighter groups shoot it out most Saturdays at high noon.

For directions to the murals, galleries, and yard art, stop at Yesterday's Restaurant, which features great burgers and a startling beer selection. 9827 Second Street, (928) 565-4251, www.chlorideaz.com.

PINBALL WIZARD

When you're in Kingman you're a mere one hundred miles from Las Vegas, a straight shot up U.S. 93, streaking across the Mojave. I'm about as low-rent a gambler as you can imagine but there is one place in Sin City where I shovel coins into machines with reckless abandon. And I'm always guaranteed a payoff, at least in terms of fun. Bonus: The money goes to a worthy cause.

It's the Pinball Hall of Fame, a collection of two hundred mostly vintage machines, lovingly restored. Picture the pinball cabinets of your youth gathered in one spot, fully functional and still costing a quarter. Picture a joyous cacophony of bells, buzzers, flapping flippers, bonking bumpers, snatches of mechanized theme songs, and the rat-a-tat of points tallied, serenading you on a nostalgia-drenched journey. The PHoF is an official nonprofit. Owner Tim Arnold funnels all excess revenue to charities, primarily the Salvation Army. And if there's a more satisfying sound than the loud thunk a pinball machine makes when you win a free game—attesting to everyone within earshot of your virility—I've never heard it. www.pinballhall.org.

Telegraph Pass
provides a high,
fine perch for
sunset viewing.

NO 34 Telegraph Pass, Yuma

This is Yuma's stair-climber trail, popular with hikers, families, and cardio-fiends alike. Great views and a good workout draw plenty of folks to this steep ascent on the edge of town. Of course, Yuma's not exactly a metropolis so even a popular trail doesn't feel overrun. I enjoyed plenty of solitude on a weekday hike.

There is no official trailhead. Just follow one of the use trails across rolling foothills to the base of the mountain. The landscape is an interesting confluence of deserts, rocky and barren, punctuated by creosote like much of the Mojave Desert. But there's also ocotillo, some barrel cacti, and even a few saguaros tucked among the cliffs, refugees of the more verdant Sonoran.

The mile hike to the base of the mountain is a nice warm-up for the main course. Once you reach the gate, the trail makes a seriously steep climb, gaining 1,200 feet in the mile to the top.

Huffing and puffing up Telegraph Pass, I pondered the evolution of how we communicate. Maybe it was the cluster of radio antennas crowning the summit. Or maybe because it seemed every other person I passed was gabbing on cell phones. That's baffling behavior to me. I don't want to deny anyone their shiny gadgets but isn't part of the joy of hiking about being temporarily off the grid? Are we that fearful of being disconnected? I long for the days of the telegram. If we were still sending wires, think how much needless chatter would be eliminated.

Consider turning off your phone and listening to what quiet sounds like. Listen to the sound of your ragged breathing, the soft crunch of footsteps on the trail, and the whoosh of a raven's wing slicing the morning sky. You won't get that in a text.

Views from the summit are spectacular, with all of Yuma laid out below. There are endless farm fields laser-leveled and shimmering green as if someone had ironed Ireland. Beyond them, the dusky curve of sand dunes and craggy mountains spill across the desert.

Where: Approaching Yuma on I-8, take Exit 14, Foothills Boulevard. Turn north, then turn right on North Frontage Road. Follow until it dead-ends, about 4.7 miles.

Cost: Free.

Difficulty: Strenuous.

Length: 4 miles round-trip.

Details: (800) 293-0071, www.visityuma.com.

Lute's Casino YUMA

First thing you notice about Lute's Casino is you're not in a casino. Then you notice you don't care because you're wandering through what resembles a mad scientist's rummage sale. Assorted collectibles gobble almost every spare inch of space. Paintings and posters cover the walls, neon signs and mannequins dangle from the ceiling. Yet people come for the burgers, not the bric-a-brac.

The veggies are so crunchily fresh you'd swear they have a garden out back—and they sort of do. Yuma hums with agricultural activity and Lute's buys local produce. Anyone with a voracious appetite, or who wants to teach their arteries a lesson, should order the Especial, a collision of taste treats that does nothing to dispel the mad scientist vibe. A cheeseburger and a hot dog are combined in an unholy, but completely delectable, union. 221 S. Main Street, (928) 782-2192, www.lutescasino.com.

Hot Tip A fleet of food trucks perch on Yuma roadsides, catering to thousands of seasonal field workers. The menus run the gamut from stingray soup to seafood ceviche to carne asada to bacon-wrapped hot dogs. Most trucks are along Eighth Street between Avenue A and Avenue D. Others are on Avenue B between First and Twelfth Streets, with another group on Fortuna Road. Check with the visitor center for the latest.

YUMA TERRITORIAL PRISON

The first things visitors see when they walk into the museum at Yuma Territorial Prison are hard, flinty eyes. No, it's not the staff having a bad day. Grim faces of some of the prison's most notorious inmates adorn one wall, including mug shots of gunman Buckskin Frank Leslie; Arizona stagecoach robber Pearl Hart; and Elena Estrada, who carved open her unfaithful lover, pulled out his heart, and threw the bloody mass into his face. Now that's an exhibit! Carved from a stony cliff above the Colorado River, Yuma Territorial Prison State Park has recently undergone a beautiful restoration. New exhibits and bold artwork paint vivid imagery of life inside the walls. Though kids find some historic sites dull, a place where they can lock their siblings in a cell, climb the guard tower, and have mug shots taken wearing prison stripes definitely isn't one of them. (928) 783-4771, www.azstateparks.com.

AGRITOURISM

Yuma's Field to Feast tour gives participants a chance to harvest fresh produce, eat a meal created from it, and get a peek at Yuma's multibillion-dollar agricultural industry. The fields show off Yuma's impressive agricultural range. If you're only interested in what ends up on your plate, the Savor Yuma tour is for you. These gastronomic adventures are progressive dinners where participants shuttle from one local eatery to the next. Both Field to Feast and Savor Yuma tours are conducted during December through March. (800) 293-0071, www.visityuma.com.

Once you finish your vegetables, you're ready for dessert at Martha's Garden Date Farm. The Yuma area is the world's largest producer of Medjool dates, a "super food" that's naturally fat free but high in fiber, potassium, and anti-oxidants. Tours are given weekdays (except in summer) if a minimum of ten people go. While many of the Medjools from Martha's Garden are shipped around the world, they're also sold on the premises. Plus, they serve a fantastic date shake. 9747 S. Avenue 9-3/4E, (928) 726-8833, www.marthasgardensdatefarm.com.

EASTERN
High Country

CHAPTER

№ 9

FOR THE ULTIMATE high country escape, travel along the Mogollon Rim and climb to the splendid fortress of the White Mountains.

When I meet people who regard Arizona as nothing but desert, I steer them to the White Mountains. Mild climate, endless forests, and a wealth of recreational opportunities draw scads of summer visitors. More than eight hundred miles of pristine rivers and streams carve up the highlands, and forty cold-water lakes sparkle like the jewelry of the nouveau riche, gaudy and glorious. Load up your fishing gear, golf clubs, and mountain bike. Pack a sweatshirt for the refreshingly cool nights and binoculars for the wildlife you're likely to see. But whatever you do, don't forget the hiking boots.

№ 35 Horton Creek, Payson

Being a waterway in Arizona is often a seasonal job. They flow as feisty as an over-caffeinated terrier during rainy times and then the rest of the year lie around in sandy pajamas. Horton Creek, though, is no part-timer. Horton goes nonstop, tumbling in a furious rush through a rich forest at the base of the Mogollon Rim. Needless to say, that combo makes for a spectacular day of hiking.

Sunlight dances across a bigtooth maple by Horton Creek.

The Mogollon Rim slashes for two hundred miles across the mid-section of the state, a soaring escarpment that serves as an abrupt boundary between parched desert and the lush green of high country, yet connecting them in a way rarely seen elsewhere. When summer blows its dragon-breath across desert valleys, residents escape to rim country.

The trail for Horton Creek starts from the Upper Tonto Creek Campground, following an old wagon road. It parallels the stream, yet is slightly removed from it. While this is a fine, shady ramble beneath ponderosa pine, Douglas fir, and an understory of juniper, oak, and maple, the water beckons. A trace trail hugs the creek bank with filament pathways connecting the two.

When a seductive cascade calls you down to the water you can clamber along the creek-side path. When you want slightly easier travel—not winding among rocks and downed logs—return to the wagon trail.

When I lived on the other side of the country, my favorite getaway was the Great Smokey Mountains. Under a verdant forest canopy, pristine, sparkling streams roared down the slopes. Crystal-throated creeks, each with a distinctive voice, would hold me enchanted for hours. I hear the

Horton Creek drops in a series of cascades through lush forest. **Opposite:** Autumn adds a dash of color to scenic Horton Creek.

same music in Horton, the ever-shifting cascades and mini-falls, the flirty slap of current against the boulders, the wet sigh of widening pools, and the chorus of trills and ripples. I spend a long time on the creek bank, reacquainting myself with the language of splash.

Fast Fact: Arizona contains the largest contiguous forest of ponderosa pines in the world, stretching from Flagstaff to the White Mountains along the Mogollon Rim.

The old wagon road and the trace trail stay in pretty close contact until the last half-mile. The wagon road gets steeper, crossing a rock-strewn segment, then launches into a few sharp switchbacks to a junction with the Highline Trail. This is today's stopping point. But first follow the sign pointing to the right to check out Horton Spring, the source of this picturesque little creek. Water gushes from the hillside, spilling over moss-covered boulders. I always take time to stop and say, "Good hustle!" to the spring before I begin the slow meander back downstream.

RIM COUNTRY MUSEUM

Explore two great exhibits for the price of one when you visit the Rim Country Museum complex. Discover a wealth of artifacts and exhibits reflecting the early history of the region, including the savage Pleasant Valley War, one of the bloodiest feuds of the American West. Admission price includes a guided tour through the museum and the Zane Grey Cabin, which was recreated after the original cabin of the western writer was lost in a 1990 fire. (928) 474-3483, www.rimcountrymuseums.com.

While this is a wonderfully refreshing summer hike, it's a favorite in autumn as well when things get gaudy up in here.

Where: From Payson, go east about 16.5 miles on Arizona 260. Turn north on Tonto Creek Road (Forest Road 289) for 0.8 miles and park in the picnic area. Trailhead is on north side of campground.

Cost: Free.

Difficulty: Moderate.

Length: 7 miles round-trip.

Details: (928) 474-7900, www.fs.usda.gov/tonto.

Buffalo Bar & Grill

PAYSON

Sitting on the main drag in Payson, Buffalo Bar & Grill is a long room with a small patio tacked on the end. The bar stretches the entire length of the room and walls are adorned with western memorabilia, bar signs, and John Wayne quotes. The menu goes beyond standard pub grub and includes soup, salads, steaks, and shrimp. Burgers are served with lettuce, tomato, onion, pickle, and mayo. On the menu, they thoughtfully print the word MAYO in bold caps so it leaps off the page, jolts you out of your reverie, and gives you a chance to come to your senses long enough to blurt out, "By all that's pure and holy, no mayo!"

I went a different route, trying a couple of their mini-cheeseburgers topped with grilled onions, a nice snacky treat with a good flavor blend. I generally steer clear of cheeseburgers. I could say it's a health thing, a few less calories consumed, but the truth is they never held me in their sway. I don't know why. A simple honest hamburger without a chapeau of melted dairy is just fine by me. But these cheesy sliders really hit the spot. 311 S. Beeline Highway, (928) 474-3900.

NO 36 Panorama Trail, Pinetop-Lakeside

I'm going to say it right up front: The name of this trail is a bit of a con. You absolutely do get big panoramas, some really nice vistas. But they're only a small part of the experience. What I remember are not the sweeping views but the stillness, the quiet moments in the patchwork of sun and shadows that fill these lush woods.

The trail cuts into the timber for a half-mile and then splits. I take the loop counter-clockwise and almost immediately spot a shortcut. Seriously. There's an official trail sign that simply says *Shortcut*. I try to recall if I've ever seen a shortcut anywhere besides a Coyote-Roadrunner cartoon. Wile E. Coyote regularly used them as part of his foolproof plans. But I continue straight ahead. Of course, I would make better time if I had used my Acme Corp. Jet-Powered Unicycle.

> **Hot Tip** Woodland Lake Park is a swath of open space practically in the middle of town. The park boasts six miles of trails, including a paved path around the lake. For Pinetop-Lakeside birders, this is a year-round hotspot.

Panorama is one of the trails developed by TRACKS, a dedicated group of volunteers. Centered in the Show Low/Pinetop-Lakeside area, 200-plus miles of trails were built in cooperation with the towns and the forest service. The network of pathways are mostly designed as loops and

FOSSIL CREEK CREAMERY

Fossil Creek Creamery is a rural throwback nestled in the tall pines of the Rim. The family farm produces artisan cheeses, lotions, soaps, and creamy fudge all made from goat milk. The five shady acres teeming with goats and llamas sits outside the hamlet of Strawberry. This is a pile-the-family-in-the-car weekend afternoon. Adults often bring a bottle of wine, make up a cheese plate, and sit on the patio while the kids romp with the baby goats.

Llama hikes are another favorite activity. The big lanky critters haul packs and equipment for visitors wishing to

explore mountain trails. Llama hikes are half-day ventures and a healthy lunch is included. 10379 W. Fossil Creek Road, (928) 476-5178, www.ranchatfossilcreek.com.

Panorama Trail consists of extensive views and shady forest.

spoked with connectors allowing for a wide range of options. For a man who loves to hike, that's practically irresistible.

I climb the shoulder of Twin Knolls with impressive views across a sea of pines. On clear days the San Francisco Peaks near Flagstaff are visible, but there must have been a smidge of haze on the horizon because I couldn't see them.

The knolls are crowned with scrub oak, and the slopes are swept bare from long ago fires. Soon the trail drops into an airy forest. For the next few miles, I meander through beautiful, mixed woodlands. Pines, junipers, and oaks with small meadows pooled around them create an ethereal park-like setting.

The trail remains level until brushing past Porter Tank and then ascends a low mesa. I love a good mesa. A mesa gives you some elevation, a lofty perch, but treats your knees with a modicum of respect. Mountains are all up or all down but a mesa is not nearly so adamant. A mesa is a mountain that's learned to relax. Sporadic views pop up through the screen of timber before I rejoin the cherry stem that leads back to the parking area.

Where: From the Lakeside Ranger District office, travel 0.2 miles southeast on Arizona 260. Turn left on Porter Mountain Road for 6 miles. The trailhead is on the left.

Cost: Free.   **Difficulty:** Moderate.

Length: 9.5 mile loop, about 7 miles if you take the signed shortcut.

Details: (928) 368-6700 Ext. 3, www.tracks-pinetop-lakeside.org.

The Lion's Den Bar & Grill

PINETOP

A guy walks into a bar. . . . No, it's not a set up for a joke, just part of my job description. But when I walk into a bar and see a woman pouring wine on a tiny flattop lined with beef patties, I wonder if I can have my mail forwarded because I may never leave. The Lion's Den was built in the 1930s and has evolved into a favorite watering hole of the locals. Inside, it's a standard sports bar with lots of wood paneling and flickering television screens. But there's also a sunny annex lined with windows and a deck around back so patrons can have the saloon experience of their choice.

I don't know when they started serving their wineburger, but it was a brilliant business decision. I watch the cook slosh a good gulp of red wine on the hot surface and it explodes in a cloud of flavored steam. I'm not sure if the seasoning comes from the wine or the flattop or a combination of both, but the tender burger absolutely melts in my mouth. 2408 E. White Mountain Boulevard, (928) 367-6050, www.thelionsdenpinetop.com.

"I wish for infinity hamburgers."

—HOMER SIMPSON

Moose Henri's

This funky little joint is unexpected in so many ways. A low-ceilinged bar filled with mismatched tables, a bevy of televisions, and lots of personality. Moose Henri's features thirty different microbrews, many from around the state. They offer beer flights so you can troll through searching for your favorites.

The menu is also slightly skewed for a sports bar, including selections like specialty kabobs, sirloins, swordfish steaks, and salmon. Their half-pound Angus beef burger is pressed out flat and wide and cradled on a velvety-soft bun. No deep fryer on the premises means no French fries. All burgers come with jalapeño coleslaw or green salad instead. Along with the standard toppings, you're also allowed to add a premium choice like bacon, guacamole, or green chile. No charge. Better dig in; you've got a lot of brews to work through. 4207 White Mountain Boulevard, (928) 368-5127, www.moosehenris.com.

CABIN IN THE WOODS

If you've ever yearned for a cabin in the woods, Cool Mountain Vacations can make your dream come true, even if it's only for a weekend or a week. They started with two cabins in the pines of Show Low. Today, they rent dozens and have used the property management company as a tool to benefit the community. They regularly run civic-minded promotions, often offering a free third night in exchange for canned goods, toys, or diapers, which are then donated. They manage a wide range of immaculate, comfortable, fully furnished cabins so you can plan everything from romantic getaways to large family outings. (928) 532-1112, www.coolmountainvacations.com.

NO 37 West Baldy, Springerville-Eagar

One advantage to being a freelance writer (i.e., grifter with a pencil) is that I follow my own schedule and can hike at off-peak times. I highly recommend this. So if you're on the fence about winning the lottery and quitting your job, put that in the Pros column. If you are gainfully employed, consider unlimbering your best fake cough for West Baldy, the jewel of the White Mountains. Because if ever there was a hooky trail, it's this one.

When you envision the perfect mountain trail, you're dreaming of West Baldy. But plenty of others share that dream, so expect loads of other hikers keeping you company on summer weekends. So call in sick to work and then TGIT! (That's "Thank God it's Tuesday" for you hooky virgins.)

The Little Colorado River serenades hikers on West Baldy Trail.

You absolutely want some solitude as you amble across these sun-smooched meadows with the music of the river sweetening the morning.

From the parking lot, the trail passes through a thin veneer of forest and then voilà! Suddenly I'm walking across a picturesque meadow near the banks of a clear-running river. For the next two miles, that's my experience. I stroll through one grassy meadow after another, each framed by forested slopes. Sunlight glints off the West Fork of the Little Colorado, a robust trout stream as birdsongs trill among the branches.

The Little Colorado loops right to the edge of the trail in places, and at other times it pulls back under the shade of the trees. After about three miles, I enter a radiant, cathedral-like forest. There's something positively ancient here, lots of big downed logs, lichen-crusted boulders, and a loamy perfume that wafts through stands of pine, spruce, and fir. This is a forest left over from

Middle Earth. I expect to see hobbits stroll past on their way to second breakfast.

The trail climbs at a steady pace, getting a bit steeper after a stream crossing. This is never a strenuous hike but you do rack up a lot of miles at high elevation. Following the contours of the mountain, the trail keeps angling upward. At one point, you pass through a large swath of trees killed by bark beetles. But after a couple of switch- backs, you climb above the ghostly grove and are back in lush timber.

A few vistas are visible from the ridge, and you also get a first glimpse of Baldy. It is not an impos- ing mountain. The actual summit is on the Apache Reservation, and access is restricted to tribal members only. Please respect their laws and don't trespass. The West Baldy Trail merges with East Baldy Trail in a saddle near the reservation border below Mt. Baldy.

From here you have a couple of options. You can

West Baldy crosses sloping meadows before climbing into the forest.

return the way you came or hike down East Baldy and use the Connector Trail, which you passed in the meadows below. That makes for a 17.5-mile hike. With a car shuttle, you can climb one trail and descend the other side. All you need to make that work is to line up a hooky-playing sidekick.

Where: From Eagar, travel west on Arizona 260 for 18 miles to Arizona 273. Turn left on 273 and drive 8.6 miles to the trailhead, which will be on the right.

Cost: Free.

Difficulty: Moderate.

Length: 14 miles round-trip.

Details: (928) 333-6200, www.fs.usda.gov/asnf.

Triggered by summer rains, wildflowers emerge along West Baldy.

TrailRiders Restaurant

EAGAR

I walked into TrailRiders with some trepidation. I'm always suspicious of joints that call themselves a "family restaurant," imagining screaming kids fighting over bowls of mashed potatoes and green bean casserole. But TrailRiders, featuring a western motif, seemed welcoming enough. After sampling the house-made chips and zesty salsa brought to the table, I knew I had chosen well.

Located just a few miles from the New Mexico border, it's no surprise they've got a couple of burgers piled high with the chiles. New Mexicans are crazy about those spicy torpedoes. There's a Jalapeño Bottle Cap burger and another topped with Hatch chiles, a milder variety named for the valley in southwestern New Mexico where they're grown. If you decide to go off script, the chicken enchiladas slathered in green sauce are terrific. 140 N. Main Street, (928) 333-1446.

"Well she got her daddy's car and she cruised through the hamburger stand now. Seems she forgot all about the library like she told her old man now."

— THE BEACH BOYS

CASA MALPAIS

An ancient pueblo from the Mogollon Culture, Casa Malpais Archeological Park perches on a high terrace amid a field of volcanic boulders near the town of Springerville. This ancient archeological site was built and occupied between A.D. 1250 and 1340. The ruins contain an astronomical observatory, a great kiva, and a natural stone stairway that leads to some breathtaking views. Both the Hopi and Zuni tribes consider Casa Malpais a sacred ancestral place. Tours of the ruins originate from the Casa Malpais Museum at the Springerville Heritage Center March through November. The museum displays beautiful artifacts excavated from the ruins of Casa Malpais. Admission to the museum is free but there is a fee for tours. 418 E. Main Street, (928) 333-5375, www.casamalpais.org.

SUNRISE PARK RESORT

I don't drive toward snow on purpose, but Arizona does get the white stuff. The beautiful part is, it doesn't snow everywhere; you have to seek it out. Sunrise Park Resort is the state's largest ski resort with sixty-five runs descending from three adjacent mountain peaks. In addition to the downhill fun, Sunrise offers 13 miles of groomed cross-country trails, a snowboard park, sleigh rides, and an awesome sledding/tubing hill. Operated by the White Mountain Apache Tribe, Sunrise has snowmaking equipment to supplement what nature provides. (928) 735-7669, www.sunriseskiparkaz.com.

Acknowledgments

THIS BOOK CAME TO LIFE with the invaluable assistance of several people. I've been a freelance writer for the *Arizona Republic* for several years and that has given me a chance to explore almost every nook and cranny of this stunning state. It is a joy and a privilege. Many of these words first appeared in the *Arizona Republic*. Thanks to the extraordinarily kind and generous Jill Cassidy, who never complains, even when every story idea I send her revolves around some combination of hiking trails and hamburgers.

Thanks also to *Arizona Highways* for the opportunity. And thanks goes to the Rio Nuevo Publishers team, especially Aaron Downey, who exhibits a bottomless reservoir of patience; to all the photographers who contributed their great work to this project; and to my sister, Susan, my longtime and most cherished burger deputy. Most importantly, thank you to my wife, Michele. I fall in love with her all over again every single day.

Finally, thanks to mustard—a darn fine condiment.

Opposite: Despite sharp and spiny fingers, the Arizona desert has an uncanny ability to steal your heart.

About the Author

The author takes a spin around the lagoons at Dead Horse Ranch State Park.

ROGER NAYLOR is a Southwest travel writer and humorist. His work has appeared in *Arizona Republic, USA Today, Go Escape, Arizona Highways, Western Art & Architecture,* and *Route 66 Magazine.* He is a senior writer for *The Bob and Tom Show,* a nationally syndicated radio program. He is the author of *Arizona Kicks on Route 66* and *Death Valley: Hottest Place on Earth.* For more information, visit www.rogernaylor.com.

Photo Credits

© ARC Photography, Tucson AZ: 75 bottom

Courtesy of Arizona State Parks: 16 bottom, 77 top

© Judi Bassett: 109 top, 109 bottom, 110 middle, 110 bottom, 113 top, 113 bottom

© Jackson Bridges/City of Page: 65 top

© Mike Buchheit: 57, 58 top, 58 middle, 58 bottom

© Edgar Callaert: 53 top

© Steve Caputo: 85 bottom left

© Barbara Carroll: 85 top

© Leland Gebhardt Photography/Chicago Hamburger Company: 73 top, 73 bottom

© Ron Chilston: 45 top

Courtesy of Cool Mountain Vacations: 110 top

© Jillian Danielson: 98 top, 98 bottom

© Keith Davis/TombstoneWeb.com: 91 bottom

© Aaron Downey: i, vi, 1, 77 bottom, 87 mid bottom

© Cale Downey: 81 top

Courtesy of Desert Botanical Garden/Adam Rodriguez: 81 bottom

© Melissa Dunstan Photography/Diablo Burger: 14

© JagFergus: 38, 40 top, 40 middle, 40 bottom, 42, 43, 44 top, 44 bottom

Courtesy of Fossil Creek Creamery: 108

Courtesy of Gouldings Lodge: 65 bottom right

Courtesy of Hassayampa Inn: 41 middle

Courtesy of The Hike House: 31 bottom

© Doug Hocking: 89, 91 top, 93 top

© John Hoskin, Rio Vaquero Photography: 23 top

Courtesy of Hotel Valley Ho: 72 bottom

Courtesy of Indian Gardens Oak Creek Market: 31 top

© Kerrick James: cover, ii, 7, 32 bottom, 34 bottom, 41 bottom, 51, 52 top, 62, 68, 70, 74 top, 75 top

© Isabel Kim: 86 bottom

© Mike Koopsen: 4, 8, 11, 20, 22 middle, 22 bottom, 24, 26, 27 top, 35 top, 53 bottom, 56, 60

Courtesy of Lake Havasu City Convention & Visitor's Bureau: 98 middle, 99 top, 101 top

© Max Latimer: 79 middle

© Bob Miller: 23 bottom, 65 bottom left, 92, 101 middle, 106

© Valerie Millett: 29, 30

Courtesy of Mini Time Machine Museum: 87 top

© Dan Minjares: 87 bottom

Courtesy of Monument Valley Balloon Company: 67

© John Morey: 5 top, 10 bottom, 12, 13, 14 middle, 14 bottom, 18 top, 18 bottom, 59 top, 59 bottom, 61 top, 72 mid bottom, 76 bottom, 80, 104, 107

© Rick Mortensen: 33, 36, 37 top, 46 bottom, 78, 79 top, 82, 86 top, 96, 102, 103 left, 114, 116

Courtesy of National Park Service: 94 top

© Roger Naylor: 16 middle, 32 top, 45 bottom, 46 top, 64 top, 64 bottom, 66, 76 top, 90, 100 middle, 100 bottom

© Joshua Noble: 99 bottom

Courtesy of Old Tucson/Marie Deamarais: 87 mid top

© Heather Otto: x, 3, 5 bottom, 10 top, 16 top, 17, 48, 50, 54, 55, 85 bottom right, 88, 94 bottom, 95 left, 112 top, 118

Courtesy of Out of Africa: 37 bottom

© Glenn Peterson: 84

Courtesy of Phoenician Resort: 72 top

Courtesy of Rancho de los Caballeros: 79 bottom

© Matt Rich: 61 bottom

© Franz Rosenberger/Prescott Office of Tourism: 41 top

© Kevin Schindler: 15

© Herberta Schroeder: 100 top, 101 bottom

Courtesy of Scottsdale Convention and Visitor's Bureau: 72 mid top

Courtesy of Sedona Chamber of Commerce: 23 middle

Courtesy of Bret Shapiro/Paradise Valley Burger Co.: 74 bottom

© Joanne Sigrist: 22 top, 25, 27 bottom, 71, 111, 112 bottom

Courtesy of Simon's Hot Dogs: 28

© Shutterstock/B&T Media Group Inc.: i, ix

© Shutterstock/Joshua Resnick: v

Courtesy of Tubac Golf Resort & Spa: 95 right

© Jim Turner: 34 top

Courtesy of Verde Canyon Railroad: 35 bottom

Courtesy of Visit Tucson: 93 bottom

Courtesy of Williams Chamber of Commerce: 47

Courtesy of Xanterra Parks and Resorts: 52 bottom

Courtesy of Yuma Convention & Visitor's Bureau: 103 right

© Ashley Zenter/Courtesy of Satchmos: 19

"The mountains are
calling and I must go."

—JOHN MUIR